The Business of Cricket

SHYAM BALASUBRAMANIAN spent his childhood in Bombay (now Mumbai). He lived a fifteen-minute walk away from the main sporting venue in the city – Wankhede Stadium. He studied in the Cathedral & John Connon School, the Indian Institute of Technology, Kharagpur, and the Indian Institute of Management, Ahmedabad. His passions are writing, cricket and decoding game tactics across sport. His travels have taken him across twenty countries, each with a different culture and customs, but each speaking one language – that of sport.

VIJAY SANTHANAM was born in Madras (now Chennai). He graduated from the University of Roorkee – now the Indian Institute of Technology, Roorkee – in 1986 and the Indian Institute of Management, Ahmedabad in 1988. In his twenty-one years of corporate (marketing) career, he worked for Godrej Soaps, Procter and Gamble and Castrol. His intense passion for cricket has led him to watch matches at the stadia in five continents, across all three forms of the game. His last corporate role was as Regional Marketing Director for Castrol, Asia Pacific and he is now a full-time writer based in Mumbai.

Shyam and Vijay have previously co-authored the book, *If Cricket Is a Religion, Sachin Is God* (HarperCollins India, 2009).

The authors would like readers' feedback at the following address:
sigreply@rocketmail.com

The Business of Cricket

The Story of Sports Marketing in India

SHYAM BALASUBRAMANIAN
VIJAY SANTHANAM

HARPER
BUSINESS

First published in India in 2011 by Collins Business
An imprint of HarperCollins *Publishers*

Building 10, Tower A, 4th Floor, DLF Cyber City, Phase II,
Gurugram Haryana – 122002, India
www.harpercollins.co.in

This edition published in Inida in 2017 by Haprer Business

4 6 8 10 9 7 5 3

P-ISBN: 978-93-5029-079-8
E-ISBN: 978-93-5136-068-1

Typeset in 11.5/14 Balaram
Jojy Philip New Delhi 110 015

Printed and bound at
MicroPrints India, New Delhi

To
Soumya and Kainaz

Contents

Prologue

The Explosive Growth of Cricket Marketing

It is hard to escape sports marketing anywhere in the world, even if you want to. Whether you are watching television, surfing the Web or trawling the mall, there is no getting away from a sports celebrity endorsing a brand.

The global sports marketing pie is worth over $113 billion and growing at 4 per cent annually, according to a report by PricewaterhouseCoopers (PwC Back on Track Report, June 2010). This figure does not include the sports goods and equipment market, which is in excess of $260 billion. A separate source (Philip Kotler, Irving Rein and Ben Shields in *The Elusive Fan*, McGraw Hill, 2006) estimated the market at $100 billion in 2006.

The PwC report gives two very useful break-ups: by source of revenue (gate – 38 per cent, media rights – 20 per cent, sponsorships – 26 per cent and merchandising – 16 per cent); and by regions (North America – 48 per cent, Europe, Middle East and Africa – 35 per cent, Asia Pacific – 15 per cent and Latin America – 2 per cent).

The growth of sports marketing in India over the last thirty-five years has been phenomenal – much higher than the global average. And unlike in the rest of the world, where sports marketing has been fuelled by sports good companies such as Nike, Adidas, Puma and Reebok, in India it has been led by one single sport: cricket. We estimate the total annual sports marketing figure in India to be ₹11,700 crore or $2.6 billion, two-thirds of which (₹7800 crore) is cornered by cricket. In our estimate, more than half of this cricket kitty comes from the Indian Premier League (IPL). We shall cover the explosive growth of the IPL in a separate chapter, but clearly the subject of sports management has become important in India, so much so that the Indian Institute of Management, Ahmedabad has recently started a course dedicated to the study of sports management!

In India, cricket has had a lion's share of the fans' interest for decades. With the launch of two cricket-dedicated channels in 2006, Neo Cricket and Star Cricket, cricket's advertising volume doubled within three years while that for other sports remained stagnant. As a result, cricket's share of sports advertising volume in India has shot up to two-thirds now (see chart). Beyond advertising, in other sports marketing aspects like sponsorships, league monies and player earnings, cricket will be easily more than two-thirds of the total Indian sports marketing.

For a long time now, especially since the 1980s, cricketers have been endorsing cars, bikes, colas, health drinks, life

Advertising Volumes in Cricket vs. Non-Cricket Sports

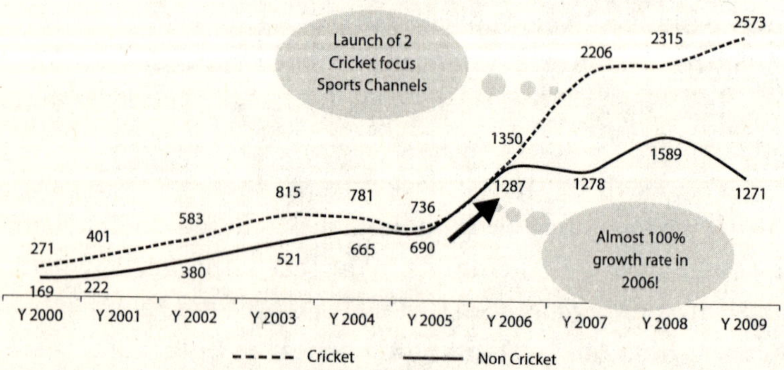

Source: TAM Sports, a division of TAM Media Research

insurance, liquor – and, of course, sports products. For example, Nike is the sponsor of the Indian cricket team's official apparel, and the Board of Control for Cricket in India (BCCI) gained a handsome fee of ₹197 crore from it over five years, 2006–10.[1] Thus, in India, Nike didn't fuel sports marketing through the BCCI but it was the other way round!

Unlike in the West, we are more of a spectator nation as far as sports goes. A friend's tongue-in-cheek comment that in India, the most physical activity in sports is using the TV remote, puts this point across. However, physical activity (or, for that matter, community activity) is gaining popularity in India – with many more people walking or jogging, going to the gym, or participating in marathons.

This book attempts to understand how sports marketing was established in the 1970s, how it expanded in the 1980s and 1990s, and finally, how it exploded at the turn of the century.

The chart on the next page shows some of the main sources of income from cricket in India today (2010–11).

Given that cricket amounts to two-thirds of the total estimated annual Indian sports marketing (as explained earlier graphically), we therefore estimate the total annual Indian sports marketing to be worth (approx) ₹11,700 crores or $2.6 billion.

So why has sports marketing become so visible now?

An answer to this question is another question: what 'ticks' in India? There are many ways to approach this question, but we take a simple but effective measure: what does India watch on TV? The answer will have to be: politics, religion, business and economics, cricket and movies. These are the subjects

[1] *Forbes*, 23 December 2005.

Main Sources of Income from Cricket

Source of Cricket Marketing Income	*Duration and Deal Amount*	*Annual Value*	*Source of the Data/Info*
BCCI-Sahara Team sponsorship	3.5 years, ends Dec 2013 ₹495 cr	₹141.43 cr ($31.43 m)	*India Today*, 31 May 2010
BCCI-Nike Official Apparel	5 years, till Dec 2010 ₹197 cr	₹39.4 cr ($8.76 m)	*Forbes*, 23 Dec 2005
BCCI-Nimbus TV rights (international matches in India)	4 years, ending 2014 ₹2000 cr	₹500 cr ($111.11 m)	ESPN Cricinfo, 15 Jan 2010
IPL Franchises	10 years (8 franchises started in '08, 2 franchises from 2011). Total $1426.92 million	₹642.11 cr ($142.7 m)	Reuters and ESPN Cricinfo
IPL Title Sponsorship (DLF Group)	5 years, 2008–13 ₹200 cr	₹40 cr ($8.89 m)	Rediff, 13 Feb 2008, *Financial Times*
IPL TV rights (Sony-World Sport Group)	9 years from 2009 ₹8200 cr	₹911.11 cr ($202.47 m)	ESPN Cricinfo, 25 March 2009
IPL Players based on ten teams and salary cap	2011	₹405 cr ($90 m)	ESPN Cricinfo, 10 Dec 2010

Source of Cricket Marketing Income	*Duration and Deal Amount*	*Annual Value*	*Source of the Data/Info*
Indian cricketers' personal brand ambassadorship fees		₹225 cr ($50 m)	Guesstimate based on individual deals publicly reported
Cricket tickets		₹1000 cr ($222.23 m)	Guesstimate
Advertising spend by brands		₹1300 cr ($288.89 m)	*Financial Express* 14 Dec 2010
Total		**₹5204.05 cr ($1156.46 m)**	
Add 50% of total as we have included only items publicly reported; we estimate 50% more due to current market value vs. original price (e.g. IPL value, private deals etc.)		₹2602.03 cr ($578.27 m)	
Gross Total Annual Cricket Marketing Income (approx)		₹7800 cr ($1750 m)	

that tick in India and have done so for decades. Ironically, till 1991, economy and business were not hot topics. Fortunately, however, New India understands their importance.

In this book, we shall focus on two areas – sports (in India, synonymous with cricket) and marketing (a core part of business). Also in focus will be the study of the biggest and latest sports marketing innovation in India, the Indian Premier League (IPL), which has interestingly fused cricket, Bollywood and business to create a multibillion dollar market. And, whether we like it or not, politics has also found its way into it, with politicians partly in charge of the BCCI and with a minister losing his post as a fallout of a controversy in the IPL.

This book has given us the opportunity to mesh together our passion for India, sports, marketing and writing. Though the book is on Indian sports marketing, we have leveraged our experience in global markets to cite principles and examples beyond India. We hope that readers will find the book both informative and entertaining.

1

Sunil Gavaskar

India's First Sports Entrepreneur

As Sunil Gavaskar was perfecting his square drive, Palmolive was perfecting his shaving.

The first time I (Shyam) heard these words was in 1974, at an air-conditioned theatre in Churchgate, when Bombay was Bombay and not Mumbai. These words were a part of a Palmolive advertisement. The reigning icon and probably the originator of sports marketing in India in its truest and most commercial sense, Sunil Gavaskar, was on the screen, shaving with Palmolive, and with each stroke of the razor, a field, a patch of the green cricket pitch, would appear on his face. These fields were a far cry from the dust bowls of the Cross Maidan and Azad Maidan we were so used to. He would lean into his perfect square drive with a stance to die for.

The film would invariably be a let-down after that.

It was a very different Mumbai then, a time when Bombelli's and Gourdons were the talk of the town, the city's art deco buildings were still contemporary, and you could get into a local train without getting killed in a stampede or worrying about bombs. Each building skirting these maidans would have teams of boys, aged eight to eighteen, playing cricket in the narrow car parking area or challenging boys from the nearby buildings, till sufficient money had been cobbled up to book that most sacred thing – a real 'pitch' at the Oval Maidan for ₹110, to play 'challenge matches'.

These pitches were virtually a sanctum sanctorum. They were the same ones that Gavaskar and Ajit Wadekar had played on. For that one day, we could play the roles of Test players and then return to the mundane realities of school exams and schedules.

On the 'official' maidan pitches, clubs like Nirlon, State Bank of India and ACC (Associated Cement Companies) would compete for shields. Rows of boys would line up for autographs from players like Ashok 'Kaka' Mankad, Eknath Solkar and Brijesh Patel. Mankad's was a cherished autograph. He was the captain of the virtually unbeatable Mafatlal team, and unlike most other cricketers who were introverted or aloof, he always seemed to enjoy himself on the field. Every bowling change of his was seen as a calculated chess move. Once you gained the reputation of being a great captain, people saw shrewdness even in the most regular bowling change!

I distinctly recall standing in queue for Wadekar's autograph. When I got to meet the man, he smiled in embarrassment and said, 'Actually I am not Wadekar, I am Bandiwadekar – do you still want the autograph?' Having invested a lot of time standing in that queue, and knowing that a Mumbai cricketer had a more than fair chance of playing in Tests for India, I asked him to sign the book. When I learnt recently that Bandiwadekar had died, I thought of that modest man and was really, really glad I had taken that autograph instead of walking away.

Where there is sport, there are fans. Where there are fans there are eyeballs and a willingness to shell out money. And where there is a willingness to spend, there is marketing.

What were the groundsmen of the Mumbai grounds but 'unofficial' entrepreneurs charging us for a sporting experience? The experience of playing on a real pitch that was greenish and not a cement one, where the ball would break unpredictably, sometimes even roll (the fearsome ghasarpatti).

The thrilling knowledge that our idols played on these wickets every weekend was an added bonus. Which cricket fan in Bombay would not cajole those extra rupees out of his parents for a compelling proposition like this?

During the period 1974–82, sport in India was not just about cricket. Cricket was a leading sport but hockey was also a national passion, with India-Pakistan matches being must-watch games. Wrestling also had an appeal, with Dara Singh being a big draw. Badminton captured the headlines of newspapers as well, with Prakash Padukone winning a number of titles in the 1978–81 period, including the All England title in 1980. Vijay Amritraj rose as an exciting men's singles prospect and was billed as the 'A' in ABC (Amritraj–Borg–Connors) the three rising stars in men's tennis in the 1970s. Michael Ferreira also won a number of international billiards titles in the 1977–81 period. With the advent of black-and-white television in the mid-1970s came the obligatory advertisements. Nearly three decades on, I can recall almost word-for-word the Complan endorsement for '*Swimmers, athletes and particularly, growing children*' – starring a now has-been Australian swimming coach – a sign that sport in India was not synonymous with cricket.

At that time, sport was great as a hobby, but not a feasible career option. There were horror stories of former greats who now lived in poverty or had turned to alcohol for solace, quite like the stories that emanate from the West Indies these days. Then something happened that added a couple of zeroes to the sponsorship of cricket in India, taking it from thousands to lakhs – India won the cricket World Cup in 1983.

After the World Cup win, the commercial importance of cricket shot up. The players who won the World Cup had hit the jackpot. There were umpteen celebrations. A less-than-melodious song, '*Bharath Vishwa Vijeyta*,' was released in which Lata Mangeshkar had to sing better than usual to cover up for Yashpal Sharma.

In the aftermath of this victory, three other factors got the sports marketing phenomenon snowballing in India.

First, the Indian cricket team won another major ODI tournament, the Benson and Hedges World Championship Cup in Australia in 1985, which was to be a precursor to the current ICC Champions Trophy.

Second, the market partially liberalized, with joint ventures between Indian and foreign companies being permitted, leading to strange sounding dual brands like Hero Honda and BPL Sanyo. This further led to an infusion of new brands seeking to grow fast.

Third, the media market exploded with family soaps like *Hum Log* and *Buniyaad*. Ramanand Sagar's *Ramayan* would give it a further boost.

Though India could not sustain its performance on the cricket field, TV media and international brands seeking to make up for lost time would become a potent combination to drive money into sports marketing. The sports market skewed towards younger players, and players like Kapil Dev and Ravi Shastri benefited from this. Ravi Shastri became the Thums Up face of the new generation. Kapil's '*Palmolive da jawab nahin*' ad is now more remembered compared to Gavaskar's original advertisement, simply because of the impact and reach of television compared to cinema. But Gavaskar, the original sports celebrity, perhaps ruing that he was born five years too early, would benefit too.

Opening His Account

Even before the World Cup win, Gavaskar understood the commercial potential of cricket at a very deep level. He was a unique phenomenon in India: a batsman-cum-entrepreneur. In the US, such entrepreneurship would be celebrated, in India it was frowned upon. Before Gavaskar, there was Farokh Engineer, the 'Brylcreem boy', and C.K. Nayudu for 'Indian Tea', sans the razor-sharp business and entrepreneurial attitude that Gavaskar brought to sports marketing.

We like to see our idols as down to earth, the same earth the rest of us have to forage in. We also want to see them as otherworldly, ascetic figures. In a nation of indigence, extravagance is looked down upon, or at least it was till the economy was liberalized. It was, therefore, good and decent for cricketers to die in poverty and drunkenness and bad for them to negotiate for more money or fixed contracts. Such logic, a product of decades of Fabian socialism, is hard to argue with.

It is necessary to perform but not everyone knows how and when to cash in. Gavaskar knew how to convert his expertise on the cricket field to business in several fields, including writing four books of surprisingly good quality. His first book, *Sunny Days*, broke all previous records of sports books in India and is pirated to this day! He also wrote *Idols*, which sold 50,000 copies[1] in its first six weeks, *Runs n' Ruins*, whose sales were poor, and *One Day Wonders*. But it was not just publishing, he flirted with movies and music as well – a prelude to what would happen with the eventual merging of the cricket and entertainment industries years later in the Indian Premier League. I remember sitting through his movie *Savli Premachi*, my sacrifice to Indian cricket! Had it been a below average movie, it would have been okay. However, it was not even that, and the vision of Gavaskar's perfect stance at the crease was replaced by that of a stranger in flared

[1] SMG, *A Biography of Sunil Manohar Gavaskar*, Devendra Prabhudesai (Rupa & Co, 2009).

bellbottom pants, wagging his finger at the audience. It was all too painful to watch. In a better move, he hosted *Sunil Gavaskar Presents*, a TV show on cricket in 1987. He has been a consistent presence in the commentary box after retirement. He was also an ambassador for a number of brands like Dinesh Suitings, Godrej Hair Dye, Cherry Blossom shoe whitener, Thums Up, Sanspareil Greenlands and Forhans toothpaste, to name a few. Then he went one step further and started the process of organizing sports marketing in India.

India's First Sports Management Company

Two years after the 1983 World Cup win, Sunil Gavaskar started a sports marketing company called Professional Management Group (PMG) with advertising executive Sumedh Shah.

PMG was to systematically professionalize sports marketing in India through four big ideas:

1. Cricket content for media: This includes syndicated articles that started in 1986, television programmes such as *Sunil Gavaskar Presents* and multimedia applications such as the Wills World Cup CD ROM and website in 1996.
2. Awards and rankings: The idea of awards was not new. Generations of Indians had been entertained (or bored) by the Filmfare Awards. This idea was extended to cricket with the Sungrace Mafatlal Cricket Awards in 1992 and the CEAT cricket ratings in 1996.
3. Sporting events and experiences: This included the 2001 recreation of the tied Test between India and Australia on its fifteenth anniversary, (they brought together the teams who had played out the tie to battle it out

again) and celebrating the twenty-fifth anniversary of the 1983 World Cup win in 2008. PMG was also to venture into commercializing golf with the organization of the McDowell's Signature Golf Club from 2002 with thirty-six golf clubs across twenty cities involving 5,000 golfers.

4. Talent management: PMG managed contracts and sponsorships for players, and created a celebrity management division in 2009. (Virender Sehwag was signed up by this division).

Between 2007–2010, PMG took its operations to the next level, when Sam Balsara, chairman of Madison Communications, and Noomi Mehta, managing director of SELVEL Advertising, bought a stake in the company. This was significant as the growth of sports marketing in India is intrinsically interwoven with that of the media, specifically the TV and entertainment industry. This is where the Indian sports landscape differs from the West, where club earnings are less dependent on TV ratings but have multiple streams of income – from collectibles, memorabilia, club magazines and a whole host of customer hospitality experiences. Post the change in ownership between 2007 and 2010, the revenues of PMG doubled.

In addition to the efforts with PMG, Sunil Gavaskar also inspired a new generation of cricketers who were more aware of their market worth and were willing to get agencies like PMG to negotiate for them. This increased the players' bargaining power with sponsors. Gavaskar himself saw his earnings per endorsement grow from ₹2000 per endorsement when he started off in the 1970s to ₹10 lakh per endorsement when he ended his playing days in the late 1980s – a 500-fold increase. A top player can expect to get ten to fifty times that amount today – in some cases, the multiple is over 5000-fold. Players were also able to get a larger share of the revenue generated by the BCCI in terms of match fees – from ₹1,000 for an entire tour in 1971 to ₹9,000 per Test by 1987, to ₹5 lakh per Test today – a 2,500-fold increase. Players have a short career and a high risk of injury. They create enormous wealth for media and advertisers. In the light of these factors, the increase in their endorsement and playing fees is fully justified.

The Bottom Line

The journey of Sunil Gavaskar from sportsman to sports entrepreneur is a fascinating one.

It all began with one thing: performance.

In his first series in 1971, in the West Indies, Sunil Gavaskar scored 774 runs in four Tests at an average of 154.80 in what was India's first series win there. This was to be followed later in the year by a series win in England, where even though his own performance was less spectacular, Gavaskar was to be associated with one of the greatest winning phases of Indian cricket. It was also important that he was a batsman, for traditionally, batsmen tend to get sponsorships more easily than bowlers. Even among bowlers, fast bowlers tend to do better than spinners, a trend peculiar to India. For a spinner to be a 'money-spinner', he needs to be a great entertainer and crowd-puller like Harbhajan Singh or Shane Warne.

Just as Gavaskar continuted to perform in a team that lost many matches after 1971, hockey player Mohammad Shahid was an otherworldly talent in a team that suffered bruising losses despite winning an Olympic gold. His stickwork was so mesmerizing that fans used to ask him if they could kiss his hands after a game! Shahid could have been a great sports marketing property, but he was in the wrong team and in the wrong game. Hockey also lacked an industry creator like Gavaskar.

There was one more reason Gavaskar captured the nation's imagination.

The 1970s was the era of the angry young man, with widespread frustration over the high unemployment rate, among other things. What the original angry young man, Amitabh Bachchan, was to Hindi cinema, Gavaskar was to cricket. He was the lone anti-establishment figure, irreverent and uncompromising, fighting to the last. His image was well-suited to the national mood of the times, when the country was looking to these anti-hero figures for some sort of respite. Even today, Gavaskar, though now a part of the establishment, at times lets down his guard and one can see the man of steel within. To that extent he is similar to Pakistan's Imran Khan or Sri Lanka's Arjuna Ranatunga, who were their respective nation's anti-establishment figures. Gavaskar's cricket philosophy and his approach in commercial matters coincides. He has often maintained a nationalist, exclusivist stance.

In an emerging market like India, a nationalist view of a sport can be limiting. For the sports market in India to grow, it cannot just be about Indian cricketers, it must make room for international cricketers and international sports like football and basketball. Non-players have as much a role to play in sports as players do, though more off-field than on. Peter Ueberroth, former chairman of the United States Olympic Committee, proved this by organizing a profitable Olympics in Los Angeles in 1984 – the first of its kind, and at a time when the term 'profitable Olympics' was an oxymoron. His Indian equivalent, Lalit Modi is also a non-player. While he finds himself in a tough position at present, it was he and not a former player who created, virtually single-handedly, the highly successful IPL.

There is less to be angry about, and more to celebrate in terms of India's rising cricket rankings and commercial relevance (over 70 per cent of cricket's revenues now come from India[2]). A broader approach is needed to keep the bandwagon rolling, which means paying the best talents the most money, irrespective of which country they belong to. A more inclusive approach must be followed to cash in on the true potential of the sports market in India. It is not enough to create wealth, it must be shared with other cricketing establishments, to facilitate an overall growth. For instance, the West Indies has given much to cricket by way of entertainment. If a small share of the TV revenues in India goes to reviving cricket in the West Indies, it is an investment in the future of cricket itself. This, of course, is based on the premise that the viewer will, sooner or later tire of watching India play Sri Lanka.

While Gavaskar drew his sustenance from Tests, in the 1980s One-day internationals would prove a bigger draw, and another player was ready to grab that opportunity. His name: Kapil Dev.

[2] Garry Linnell, *Daily Telegraph*, 2 February 2008.

2

Kapil Dev

Charisma, Rivalries and the Transition to TV

While Sunil Gavaskar created a foundation for a sports market in India, Kapil Dev took over the mantle in the 1980s, taking the value of endorsements from the tens of thousands to lakhs of rupees.

Three factors were crucial in the Kapil Dev era of sports marketing. The first, and most obvious, was his charisma; the second, rivalry; and the third, Doordarshan.

Kapil Dev had an unusual charisma about him. Previous cricket role models like Pataudi, Engineer, Jaisimha and Gavaskar had been English-educated and from big cities. Kapil Dev was the classic 'outsider', a break from the self-perpetuating circle of big cities. What Dhirubhai Ambani did for Indian business in the 1970s, Kapil Dev did for Indian cricket in the 1980s. In their own way, both ventured out-of-the-box. Chandigarh boy Kapil Dev opened the door for cricketers from the smaller *Bunty-aur-Babli* towns. Today, Dhoni, Munaf Patel and Zaheer Khan have Kapil Dev to thank for shattering the glass ceiling.

I (Shyam) remember being told by my parents, who were to meet the Indian cricketers for dinner at the Taj Coromandel in 1987, that the only person who stood up to shake hands with all the guests was Kapil Dev. These things do not go unnoticed by sponsors either. They need a brand ambassador who will connect with consumers and customers. An ambassador who scowls silently in the corner of a room wishing he wasn't there, is of no use at all in building a relationship with customers.

Kapil Dev came in when sports marketing was in a transitional phase: action was shifting from cinema and radio to television. Television is an audiovisual medium. Charisma and rivalry do not have to be explained as in radio; people can see it.

Kapil Dev was fortunate in having played in the company of three other great all-rounders: Ian Botham, Imran Khan and Richard Hadlee. Thus even if India and New Zealand did not have any historic rivalry to speak of, the Kapil-Hadlee dimension made their clashes worth watching. Each of these four personalities was larger than life. They were class cricketers who played to win and attacked relentlessly on field. Kapil played 131 Tests of which 46 (or 35 per cent) involved Botham, Imran and Hadlee. Just over a third of his career was therefore highlighted by these marquee contests within a contest. In the One-day arena, out of 225 One-dayers, 49 (or just over 21 per cent) involved one or another of Kapil's rivals.

This made these contests watchable, even if the respective national teams of these four all-rounders were not always brilliant in the 1980s. All those who endured England opener Chris Tavare in 1980–81 will know what we are talking about.

All these personalities were associated with big wins. Kapil Dev had a home series win (along with some great batting by Gavaskar) against Pakistan in a series that we were expected to lose in 1979–80; a memorable away win in England in 1986; and, of course, the World Cup in 1983. Imran had the World Cup win in 1992, home wins against India and Australia in 1982–83 and, remarkable away performances in the West Indies when the latter were still a formidable force in 1987–88. Botham dominated the 1981 Ashes in an all-round way that has seldom been seen; perhaps Andrew Flintoff in 2005 comes closest to it. Hadlee had away Test series wins in Australia (1985–86) and England (1986). During his era, New Zealand was one of the toughest 'home teams' to beat. From 1980–1990, with Hadlee in the team, New Zealand remained unbeaten at home, winning eight out of twelve Test series played during that period.

These rivalries were riveting. On one memorable occasion in March 1990 in Wellington, Hadlee was virtually unplayable, taking 2 for 27 while Kapil's rearguard knock of 46 off 38 balls took India to 221. While chasing, New Zealand seemed out of it till Hadlee came in and hammered 46 runs off 37 balls before he was bowled by Kapil, giving India a nail-biting one-run win. Such all-round mortal combats gave these matches a sense of frisson, which keeps them fresh in one's memory even twenty years on.

Proof of Kapil's brilliance, not that one is required, is this: If a wicket did not fall for any length of time, the cry of 'we want Kapil' would echo around the stadium.

Kapil's charismatic personality and on-field brilliance made him an obvious choice for brands such as Boost, Kinetic motorcycles and BSA–SLR bicycles, which needed to communicate energy and dynamism. Also, Kapil had a pan-India appeal, because he was not a metro-only personality.

Kapil's career flourished at a time when, thanks to the 1982 Asian Games in the country, television was expanding in the country. It is exciting to look at viewership figures (see chart) during Doordarshan's expansion phase and Kapil's career.[1]

[1] *The Diffusion of Television in India*, Singhal, Doshi, Ropers and Rahman, Media Asia Volume 15(4) 222–9, 1988

Kapil's Career and DD's Expansion

1977	Kapil takes 11 wickets in a first class match and books his ticket to the Irani Cup and with it the Pakistan series	TV viewers: 9 million
1983	World Cup (broadcast live with one break in transmission) – India, captained by Kapil, wins	TV viewers: 30 million
1985	India win Benson & Hedges World Championship in Australia	TV viewers: 60 million
1987	Kapil plays arguably his best innings in the tied Chennai test against Australia	TV viewers: 80 million

The big insight is that charisma, rivalries and media reach expand the sports market.

This applies to other sports in other markets as well, not just cricket in India.

To expand on this let's start with a question.

Who is the current World Heavyweight Boxing Champion?

Very few people will be able to answer the question but during the Muhammad Ali era, the answer to this question would have been a lot easier. For Ali, was a multifaceted and charismatic personality. Apart from being a champion boxer, he was also an 'unofficial' civil rights leader and a shrewd promoter of his own fights.

It helped that Ali had meaningful rivals like Frazier, Liston, Norton and Foreman. The Ali-Frazier rivalry is legendary. When Ali lit the Olympic flame in 1996, Frazier is said to have wanted to 'push him into it'. When Ali was active as a boxer (1960s and 70s), heavyweight boxing was the event to watch. There are many intriguing sidelights to the Ali-Frazier rivalry but one interesting aspect is that Frazier lent Ali money when the latter was banned for opposing the Vietnam war. Frazier also helped Ali return to boxing. The reason was not pure goodness of heart. Frazier would earn about half-a-million dollars for a fight but five times that amount for a fight with Ali. Commercial interest and pride would have dictated that he lend a helping hand to his arch rival.

By the 1980s, heavyweight boxing had lost spectator interest, which had shifted to the welterweight and middleweight categories.

The reason again was charisma and rivalries.

The real successor to Ali was not Larry Holmes but Sugar Ray Leonard who took on the peoples' champion mantle. Another 'pretty' boxer like Ali, Sugar Ray had meaningful rivalries with Duran, Thomas 'The Hitman' Hearns and 'Marvellous' Marvin Hagler.

This drove boxing lovers away from the heavyweight to the welterweight and middleweight categories. The fight between Hearns and Hagler in 1985 is not a byline to the Sugar Ray Leonard story but is also the stuff of legend. In what is now reverentially referred to as 'The War' by boxing fans, the two fighters went at each other toe to toe from the first round. The fight lasted eight minutes. But the sheer ferocity of the fighters has made the contest unforgettable. Classics do not have to go fifteen rounds, sometimes two-and-a-half are sufficient.

Today heavyweight boxing is in some sort of crisis, lacking both charisma and rivalries.

The photo of Kapil Dev lifting the World Cup after the victory at Lord's is an enduring visual, one that is resurrected every four years to revive fans' hopes. Much of the final between India and the West Indies was seen live (although there was a break in transmission during the game as the satellite went out of range). This single moment came to be what Philip Kotler, Irving Rein and Ben Shields called a 'brand forming moment'[2]. These are moments 'that instil in the fan a strong sense of what constitutes the brand.' So momentous was this World Cup-winning moment that despite several subsequent reversals, people continued to have faith in the team.

Even the Palmolive mantle was now passed on from Gavaskar to Kapil Dev, with the new tag line, '*Palmolive da jawab nahi*'. Advertising agencies would now milk his small-town origin to the hilt – giving Kapil a Hinglish catch phrase to widen their product's appeal. Pepsi, with their product launch in India were to do much the same with their '*Yehi hai right choice baby*' advertisement with none other than Kapil. There was more to the Pepsi launch in India than just Kapil. There were also unforgettable advertisements (1990–1993) with Remo, Aamir Khan, Aishwarya Rai and Mahima Chaudhary. Cricket and Bollywood were used, but in separate advertisements without an overlap.

Over the years, Kapil has transitioned from consumer-to-consumer to business-to-business marketing, from being a player to being an entrepreneur with a Teflon image that seems to absorb every controversy. He is every bit as entrepreneurial as Gavaskar – for example, when Gavaskar launched PMG, Kapil followed soon with Dev & Dev, and Dev Features. The rivalry between Sunil Gavaskar and Kapil Dev over captaincy of the Indian cricket team was to extend to the field of business as well. Dev ventured into real estate, opened hotels and restaurants, established the Dev Musco Lighting Pvt Limited company for stadium lighting and even played cameos in a few Hindi films. He has managed his brand image well, as the straight talking, down-to-earth guy who is at the same time a smart negotiator – an image that works well in the Indian market. Kapil Dev's small-town rusticity gave him

[2] *The Elusive Fan*, McGraw Hill, 2006.

a few brownie points with the Indian consumer, as against Gavaskar's urbane, English-elite image.

The Indian sports market benefited from this Gavaskar-Kapil rivalry. As a consequence, intended or unintended, bargaining power for players increased significantly.

By 1992 there was real money off the field with sponsorships. The marquee names were able to swing bigger deals. Kapil was reportedly getting ₹10 lakh a year for a three year deal with Pepsi in the early 1990s. A far cry from the ₹2000 that Pataudi got for his signature on a bat in the late 1960s.Cricketers were getting a better deal, which reflected their market value.

While Kapil Dev took the sports marketing numbers into multiples of lakhs, his successor, Sachin Ramesh Tendulkar would take it to the next level.

As the commercial goes, *Sachin aala re.*

3

Sachin Tendulkar

The God of TRPs

When I (Vijay) started my career in marketing in 1988, we had only two TV channels in India, both from Doordarshan (DD-1 and DD-2). Of course, DD-2 was only for the metros, and I was fortunate to live in one of these. However, in terms of sports coverage, my experiences of DD's goof-ups are too many to recount. For the sake of the young, IPL-fed, 100-plus-TV-channels generation, I shall illustrate this with a couple of examples, so that they can feel the misery that sports fans of my generation were subjected to.

The Break Point: Sports on DD

In 1982, in the midst of a telecast of the classic tennis drama of a Wimbledon men's final, McEnroe vs. Jimmy Connors, viewers were forced to watch news bulletins, butchering the thrill of a five-setter. And I still deeply regret that McEnroe lost that final. If you have been a McEnroe fan, then you can understand why; he ought to have won four straight Wimbledon finals, from 1981 to '84.

Let's paint a more vivid picture:

Year:	1995
Contest:	World Chess Championship
Contenders:	Vishwanathan (Vishy) Anand vs. Garry Kasparov, game 17

Anand desperately needed to win with black to stay in the match and played a brave d5 in response to Kasparov's e4, taking the game to a fascinating position. At 4.30 a.m. sharp DD cut the coverage! This time, it was not because of a break for news (not to be confused with 'Breaking News' of today's channels), but because DD had bought the coverage for only four hours of the game. The TV screen just went blank – without apology, without reason.

Doordarshan played spoilsport when it came to cricket coverage too. It was tough to decide which was worse – the commentary or the camera work – as the cameraman would invariably miss the action, or pan the camera and show the off-side while the batsman had played a shot on the on-side.

While we did enjoy the occasional well-covered cricket match on TV in the 1980s – for example, the 1983 World Cup (though the final was interrupted by DD for news, of course), the 1985 Benson & Hedges World Cup Championship in Australia (and what joy it was to watch the Australian channel 9 coverage!), it was only from 1991, with the birth of the Cable and Satellite (C&S) channels, that we got regular good-quality coverage.

The economic liberalization in 1991 and the subsequent rise of India at the global scale have been well documented. The amazing transformation of the electronic media scene is a good example of it. The BCCI understood (from the 1983 World Cup win and the subsequent co-hosting of the 1987 World Cup) that there was much more money in One-day matches than in Test matches. At this point, we need to acknowledge the role of Jagmohan Dalmiya (BCCI President and then ICC Chairman), perhaps the man who understood most what financial gains BCCI could make.

A list of matches played by different countries between 1 January 1990 and 31 December 1999 bears this out:

Test and One-day Break-up (1990–99)

	Test matches	*One-dayers*
India	69	257
Australia	108	225
England	107	135
West Indies	81	195

Source: Derived from 'Match and Series Archive' of ESPN-Cricinfo.

As Test match enthusiasts, our view is that the BCCI, driven by commercial considerations, perhaps arranged thirty-five Test matches less – and about fifty One-dayers more – than what was required during this decade. But few complained – because for media buyers and sellers, marketers et al, the value of higher TRPs for ODIs made the decision a no-brainer.

The BCCI also understood the importance of state cricket associations enjoying their share of the revenues, so the ODI matches were held across the country. In parallel, the board cultivated 'associate countries' like Kenya, Ireland and Bangladesh. Bangladesh became a full member of the Indian Cricket Council (ICC), all thanks to the BCCI's influence, as a majority of the money in the game came from India: today this figure has gone upto approximately 70 per cent.[1] As Pataudi said recently, 'If ICC is the voice of the game, BCCI is the invoice!' Just as each state association counts in the BCCI elections, each country's vote counts in the ICC affairs. Over time, India became the powerhouse of cricket and the BCCI became the 'ATM' of the game globally.

[1] *Daily Telegraph*, Australia, 2 February 2008

While the BCCI's focus on money and power have dented the game in several respects, overall, the last two decades have seen Indian cricket marketing soar with many positives: better stadia (for instance Nagpur); better coverage and commentary (as against the DD days), match timings being kept with Indian audiences in mind (the way the European audience gets to watch football at a time suitable to them), just to mention a few. However, it is important to ensure that money is earned legitimately and then eventually used productively and in the right places, like in sports infrastructure, training and mentoring.

A Great Delivery Vehicle Arrives

Clearly, the horoscope of Indian sports marketing was looking promising at the start of the 1990s – with economic liberalization, the TV media boom, a financially savvy board, the fact that many companies could afford the marketing budgets required to advertise and promote their brands as these became more widely available (a corollary of having a more open market), and a happier consumer with more purchasing power than before. But even with all this, Indian sports marketing needed a great delivery vehicle to ride piggyback on. Enter Sachin Tendulkar, who debuted (internationally) in 1989.

In marketing parlance, while the medium is very important, the message is even more so. That is why marketers understand the real power of great creative ad campaigns or promotions. In the 1990s, cricket was the platform of Indian sports marketing (within it the 'One-day' format was more popular), TV was the main media, and Tendulkar was undoubtedly the creative magic potion. In reality, all through that decade and the next, more than any other player, he has driven cricket marketing in India. Before we elaborate on this, we need to make an honourable mention of Mark Mascarenhas, the head of WorldTel, who understood Sachin Tendulkar's commercial value and prospects. In a milestone in Indian sports marketing overall and specifically in the area of professional player management, he signed a deal with Sachin for a guaranteed sum of ₹31.5 crore ($7.5 million) in 1996 for five years. Within three years, WorldTel raised ₹42 crore ($10 million)! In the next five-year deal, Sachin was guaranteed a sum of ₹100 crore (over $20 million). As we shall see in the ensuing examples, Sachin thoroughly deserved this amount.

Over the last two decades, the India-Australia Test series have been fought bitterly, have touched great highs in terms of quality, and frankly, have been more competitive than the Ashes or even the India–Pakistan clashes. However, during the India–Australia Test in Nagpur in 2004, ticket sales were marginal. Australia had won the first Test in Bangalore and the last day of the second Test in Madras had been washed out by rain – Indian fans believed they were robbed of a certain win. Though the 0–1 series status was one reason for poor ticket sales, the main one was that Sachin was injured, had missed the first two Tests, and fans feared that he might not play in Nagpur. However, the Nagpur association saw its gate sales triple in one day when Tendulkar was declared fit for the Test on 26 October 2004. This vouches for the SRT effect on the box office.

The second example is the 1996 World Cup, hosted by India, Pakistan and Sri Lanka. That it was a sell-out in India had a lot to do with Sachin's performance: 127* vs. Kenya, 70 vs. West Indies, 90 vs. Australia, 137 vs. Sri Lanka, 3 vs. Zimbabwe, 31 vs. Pakistan (quarter final) and 65 vs. Sri Lanka (semi final) – a mind-blowing 442 runs overall, a record for a player in a single World Cup, broken only in 2003, by Sachin himself.

With so many channels available today to the viewer, viewership has been split and fragmented. So, a TRP (TV Rating Point) of 5 is huge. Even a TRP of 1 (1 per cent of the 113 million TV sets) is very important and most often profitable – it means over a million homes watched a particular telecast. In the last decade (2000–2010), the number of TV sets in the country has grown dramatically, by 42 per cent.[2] Keeping this in mind, a TRP of 5 in India today (with more than one person per TV set) is much more than the whole of Singapore (total population around 5 million).

More interestingly, for the advertiser, the cost of a TRP has grown much more dramatically – it is almost six times what it was a decade back! The cost of a TRP per 10 seconds on TV for cricket matches jumped from around ₹10,000 in the 2001–03 period to almost ₹60,000 in 2009.[3] Here's what the math tells us: the number of TV sets grew by 42 per cent over the decade (2001–2009) but the cost of a TRP has grown by 500 per cent, making advertising on TV during cricket matches more and more expensive.

A good example of how Sachin's magical touch sends TRPs skyrocketing is the 2009 India–Australia One-day series at home. With the series tied at 2–2, perhaps the most important match of this series was the match in Hyderabad on 5 November. Tendulkar enthralled the viewers with an enchanting 175 (even though India lost the match and eventually the series as well). An article in *The Times of India* dated 13 November 2009 read: 'The Mumbai maestro's sensational 175 off 141 balls last week sent the television ratings soaring to a whopping 7.1, the highest in ODI matches in recent years... The first match had TRP of 3.6, followed by

[2] 79 million in 2001 to 113 million in 2009, IRS

[3] Courtesy Madison World and ESPN– Star

4.9 and 5.9 in the second and third matches and the average TRP in the first five matches was 5.51.'

Of course, all records in terms of TRPs and cost of media were shattered during the 2011 World Cup final between India and Sri Lanka in Mumbai. The average rating of the match (telecast on Star Sports, Star Cricket, and Doordarshan) was 23.2, peaking at 35.9.[4] And the cost of 10 seconds on TV shot up to an unprecedented ₹20–24 lakh.[5]

The Toothpaste Wars

This case study is significant as it shows that one of the greatest turnarounds in India's brand wars – that of Colgate's market share and its confidence, its brand equity and fortunes – was anchored by Sachin Tendulkar.

For most of the twentieth century, until 1990, Colgate was in a state of undisputed leadership in the toothpaste category. But post the economic reforms of 1991, a flood of new brands had led to a sharp decline in Colgate's profit and its confidence. To get the right perspective on the Colgate story, we spoke to Sandeep Goyal, chairman of Dentsu, who was managing the advertising agency Rediffusion when it had the Colgate account in the 1990s.

Colgate in India was known for its 'Big Red' Colgate, the white toothpaste with the 'ring of confidence' visual that was recommended by dentists. This product had virtually created the toothpaste market in India and in the 1990s had a leadership share of over 60 per cent. The total oral care market was about ₹2000 crore and half of it fell under the toothpaste category, the rest being toothpowders, which were largely popular in rural India.

[4] *The Economic Times*, 7 April 2011

[5] *Business Standard*, 5 April 2011

However, Colgate witnessed a sharp loss of market share from 60 per cent to 38 per cent and loss of confidence and brand equity in the period 1990–1997.

Colgate's competitor, Hindustan Lever, had relaunched its brand Close-Up in 1989, with three things to differentiate it from the jaded, though trusted, brand of Colgate. The first was that it was a coloured gel with two options – red and blue. The second was that it targeted the younger demographic with a relevant catch phrase '*Close-Up is for Close Ups.*' Finally, the packaging was new and sleek and, in a smart move, Unilever applied their sachet-packing technology for shampoos to toothpastes, to attract the low-income group and rural consumers.[6]

This relaunched brand of Close-Up, with new strategies of brand positioning, gained market share rapidly and within two years, had a 17 per cent share. As if things weren't bad enough for Colgate, Hindustan Lever relaunched another brand, Pepsodent, and placed it as a more scientific take on germ removal. In a TV commercial in 1997, Hindustan Lever claimed that Pepsodent was 102 per cent better than Colgate at fighting germs. By now Colgate was on the ropes and its market share had fallen to about 38 per cent, while Pepsodent's had grown to 6 per cent from almost nothing.

Colgate's response to this existential challenge was strategically brilliant. In 1993, they launched 'Colgate Total', a super premium brand priced twice as much as Colgate Dental Cream, which was ₹12 at the time. The product had a unique ingredient, triclosan, which could protect the teeth and gums from cavities and gingivitis for upto twelve hours after brushing. And in a masterstroke, they signed up Sachin Tendulkar as the brand ambassador in 1998 and leveraged

[6] http://www.indianexpress.com/fe/daily/19990421/fle21069.html

him for Colgate Total. It also increased its marketing spend on toothpastes by 50 per cent in the fiscal year 1998.

Colgate Total quickly gained a share of 3 per cent (closer to 6 per cent in value terms as it was double the price of Colgate Dental Cream). More importantly, this entire initiative with Sachin Tendulkar changed the image of Colgate from a fading brand to once again, the most relevant, or the most 'total' product in the toothpaste market. The decision to make Sachin the face of the brand was based on his image as a complete cricketer, or the most 'total' batsman – a perfect fit with the brand's benefits, as it also banked on his credibility in the eyes of the consumer. In fact, when mothers (since this product was a family toothpaste) were asked which cricketer they would want their sons to emulate, a staggering 99 per cent chose Sachin as the role model for their children.

There were more successful initiatives (e.g. 'herbal') but the final grand slam was the relaunch of Colgate Dental Cream in 1999, with a memorable tagline, '*Mera Colgate*', which reminded consumers of the brand they had almost forgotten, and brought them back in droves, with a 10 per cent share gain. By 2000, the Colgate brand had regained its original share in the market of 60 per cent.[7] While all the various brand initiatives helped, Colgate Total was the most crucial in the turnaround – in terms of brand equity, the start of regaining market share and company confidence.

Though one can't fully credit Sachin for the resurrection of Colgate as a brand, one cannot doubt that his presence gave a massive boost to the brand through sports marketing. Sachin had a phenomenal year in 1998, averaging 80.87 in Tests (including helping India beat Australia) and 65.31 in One-dayers (a strike

[7] http://www.moneycontrol.com/company-facts/colgatepalmoliveindia/history/CPI

rate of 102), scoring twelve international centuries in the process (including two very memorable innings in Sharjah). Would Colgate have have been so successful had they chosen any other Indian player? Would they have succeeded if they had not unleashed the kind of innovation they did? The credit goes to the Colgate team and the advertising agency, Rediffusion, for making this remarkable turnaround.

Now most people think that players put advertisements ahead of their cricket and that's why their game suffers – at least this is the refrain every time India loses. But in the opinion of advertising expert Sandeep Goyal, choosing an ambassador for a brand is risky because the player in question will always prioritize cricket over advertising and one also cannot guess what the competition is going to come up with. Goyal, who has worked with Kapil, Sachin and Dhoni, says that in all three cases, cricket took precedence; frequently a shoot that needed three days would have to be crammed down to half a day.

Tendulkar is not just one of the greatest cricketers ever and the biggest brand ambassador globally among cricketers or across sportsmen in India, but is also an industry, an ecosystem. At the peak of Amitabh Bachchan's career, he was called 'the one-man industry' in the context of Bollywood. There were several people feeding off the Big B effect. It is true in the case of Sachin Tendulkar in sports marketing.

First there are the local state associations whose gate receipts are boosted by Tendulkar's presence – this is similar to the 'box office collection' aspect. Then there are all those who feed off the incremental effect on TRPs when Tendulkar plays – media companies, state associations (who also get their share), and sponsors.

Finally there is a link between Sachin and the collective self-image of Indian cricket fans and fanatics. We tried to capture the concept with the following diagram:

The Tendulkar Ecosystem

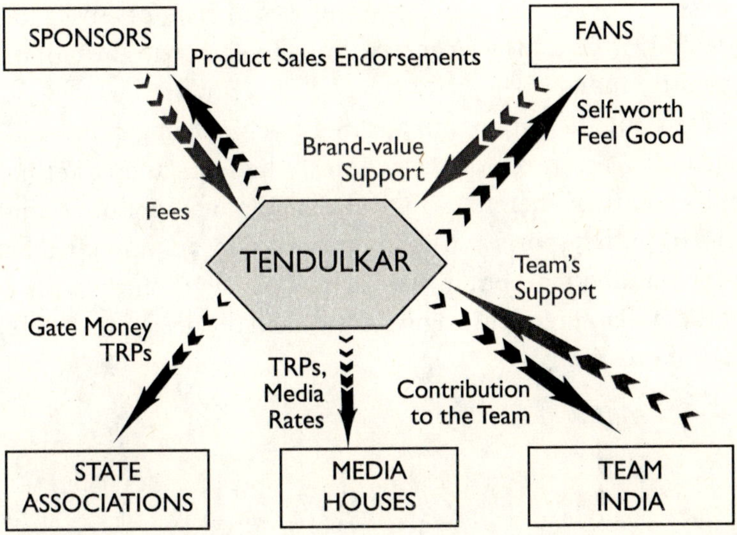

We believe that Sachin Tendulkar has been the epitome of a new, proud India, post-liberalization. Brand Sachin evokes important positive characteristics like *total/complete* (as explained in the Colgate Total case), *trust* (because of his on-field and off-field behaviour), *durability* (because of an incredible career duration in international cricket – twenty-one years and counting), *performance* (because of his contribution to the team, his achievements and records), and his appeal across gender, age and region. No wonder 'Brand Sachin' has great equity and companies queue up for his endorsement.

The 1960s were the era of the stylists – Jaisimha and Durrani in cricket, Rajesh Khanna in films and the box-wallah companies (e.g. British companies like ITC, ICI) with their silver teapots. As mentioned in the previous chapters, the 1970s saw the rise of angry, young 'anti-establishment' men – Amitabh and Gavaskar. The 1980s saw the rise of 'outside the establishment' men like Kapil Dev in cricket and the

Ambani family in business. The 1990s saw a liberated India – SRT in cricket and the likes of Infosys in business. What of the 2000s? Perhaps we can say it has given rise to the cult of celebrity India?

It is tough to imagine another Sachin being born and becoming the pivot of the whole Indian sports marketing industry. It is, therefore, logical that the next big quantum leap of Indian sports marketing came not by an individual or a set of individuals but by way of a whole new concept – that of the Indian Premier League, as we shall discuss towards the end of the book.

4

The Winner Takes All

Appeal of Foreign Sportspersons

In their book *The Winner-Take-All Society*, the economist Dr Robert H. Frank of Cornell University and public policy expert Philip J. Cook of Duke University write about a society where a few winners walk away with a lot while the rest are left with little. This is deemed a natural consequence of technology and market advantages. This idea holds true for sportspersons as well. Today players get rewarded in proportion to their overall status in the game and the eyeballs they attract. As a result, a few big players – quite literally, 'winners' – get special attention from the media and sponsors while a vast majority – specially those engaged in sports not as fancied as cricket – is left with little to fall back on. The big implication of this is that the 'winning' professionally-marketed sports, like cricket in India or football in Europe, will get the lion's share of the endorsements. Even within the winning sport, the better performers will get disproportionately rewarded. That's why you see the same faces again and again on TV even though there are eleven players on the field for the Indian team. This is a massive change from the pre-television era of the 1960s, when all sportsmen (including cricketers) relied on local company or government jobs for financial security.

There is something poignant about this change. It speaks of the very real battle between mainstream and community sports. The 'winner-take-all' phenomenon plays a pivotal role in the decline of smaller community and grassroots sports played by college teams and railway and army clubs. Though some markets like the US are sufficiently large and localized to allow for community sports (for example, college basketball), as a trend they are getting increasingly less competitive. This means that folk sports such as kho kho and kabaddi, like folk dancing, are probably heading towards becoming tourist attractions only.

On the positive side, it means people routinely get to see the best players perform at the flick of a button – for instance, Federer vs. Nadal – rather than having to go to a distant venue once a year to watch Nandan Bal play Enrico Piperno.

When brands like Gillette, with taglines such as '*The best a man can get*', conduct their research, they tend to ask: 'Who is considered (in the country-specific market) the best performer in a particular sport?' And surely, the answer will not be the local hockey player but some of the big names mentioned earlier.

This explains why international sportspersons are being integrated into the marketing campaigns in India, a trend that will only increase. For instance, there has been an unprecedented rise in the number of international sportsmen since the first season of IPL in 2008. In the two-day IPL auction in 2011, of the 124 players 'sold', a staggering 78 were international players.

One of the first instances of foreign participation in Indian sports marketing was in the 1960s, when Farokh Engineer became the 'Brylcreem Boy' for India, replicating a global campaign made famous by the likes of Denis Compton and Keith Miller. Perhaps this was the beginning of globalization of cricket marketing as we know it. In the 1970s, Andy Roberts, the West Indian fast bowler, and Tony Greig, the South African-born English cricketer, starred in an advertisement for

Erasmic blades (then owned by Lever's); these print ads were used only in India. And during the 1987 World Cup, sponsored by Reliance, several international stars like Viv Richards and Allan Border featured in ads for Vimal Suitings.

Imran's Freshness Soap

Imran Khan starred in a mainstream commercial ad in India for Cinthol soap, with the catchphrase '*Imran's freshness soap*', in the late 1980s. His popularity then was at its peak as he was among the 'Big Four' all-rounders who brought to cricket a charisma not seen since Keith Miller had flown a fighter aircraft in World War II and befriended Princess Margaret. The Imran Khan campaign, which appeared on television, in print and on point of sale (checkout display), was a terrific success. Normally, companies had to pay for visibility in stores. However, in the case of this ad, the dealers themselves offered the company ₹10 per poster to display it in their stores. Cinthol, owned by Godrej Soaps, was a strong but traditional brand with deep loyalty in south India for the 'regular' 100-gram version of the soap. Cinthol 100-gram was a brand used by 40+ males, especially in Tamil Nadu, as a soap plus deodorant. The deodorant benefit was always powerful in the South. The dandies of Madurai would wear ringlets of flowers around their wrists on an evening out. What Imran did was make the brand cool and contemporary with the 'new' 75-gram line.

The Imran campaign was a landmark campaign for various reasons. It challenged the belief that to connect with the Indian market, an Indian brand ambassador was needed. Here was a brand ambassador who was from Pakistan, a neighbour with whom relations have always been tense. It took courage for Godrej Soaps to go ahead with this in 1986, for at any moment, relations between the two countries could have deteriorated, leading to negative repercussions on the campaign. Its success demonstrated the open-mindedness of the Indian consumer to international sportsmen as brand ambassadors. On the other hand, a Gavaskar or a Kapil Dev in a TV ad campaign in Pakistan or Australia, would probably not work. It is intriguing to note that the use of international sports stars in campaigns in India was pioneered by Indian companies like Godrej Soaps, Reliance (the Vimal campaign) and Parle (Thums Up) in the 1980s more so than multinationals.

It also established the importance of celebrity appeal – a phenomenon that would reach its zenith in the 2000s. In the 1970s, advertising sold products merely on the basis of the benefits it offered to the consumer. Post 2000s, advertising sells products on the basis of the celebrity that endorses them. In retrospect, the 1980s and '90s can be seen as the transition into the celebrity era. All celebrities will not guarantee sales, the high performers or winners are a better bet. This is an unintended consequence of the winner-take-all society, that you have to see the same endorsers for different products rather than unique endorsers for each product.

The Cinthol campaign widened the appeal of cricket to include women, for obvious reasons – Imran's star/sex appeal. As women are the primary decision makers in the purchase of consumer goods such as soap, this was very significant. Cricketers like Pataudi, Gavaskar and Kapil Dev had already proved that it was possible for a cricketer to have cross-gender appeal – but they were all Indian sportsmen. With Imran, we saw for the first time that an international cricketer could have crossover and cross-gender 'pin up' appeal.

Sam Balsara, chairman and managing director of the advertising agency, Madison World, who worked on the Imran campaign, explained how the ad originated: 'Parmeshwar Godrej came up with the idea of leveraging charismatic, male achievers as Cinthol models – Imran Khan, and then Vinod Khanna. She managed to convince others and overcome concerns about having a Pakistani model for an Indian brand.'

If Lux was 'the beauty soap of film stars', Cinthol made 'the macho male star' image its own.

There is a link between the campaigns for Brylcreem, Erasmic and Godrej. In 2007 Godrej was to acquire the Erasmic shaving range from its British owners Keyline (who had acquired the brand in 1990–91). In 2008 Godrej Sara Lee was to relaunch Brylcreem in India with the latest Brylcreem boy, M.S. Dhoni. Brylcreem was also relaunched in the UK with another South Africa-born English cricketer, Kevin Pietersen, in an echo of the Tony Greig endorsement. In a sense, the circle of Brylcreem, Erasmic and Godrej is complete.

Global sports marketing alliances, events and the media have also led to an increased participation of international sportspersons in Indian sports marketing. Just as globalization of world economies has resulted in a coming together of companies and brands, it has led to a globalization of sportspersons in the world of sports marketing. When large sums are paid for rights to an event or player, it makes sense to flog the property in as many markets as possible. Therefore, if Vodafone has a link with Lewis Hamilton through Formula 1, he will play a keen role in marketing activities in India for their joint venture with Essar. In the first chapter on Gavaskar we explained how the rights fees for a sporting endorsement had gone up by an inflation unadjusted factor of 5000. Even where tournaments are concerned, the rights increase is of this magnitude. Vodafone Essar paid ₹45 crore for the sponsorship rights for the World Cup in 2011, but this included media and other benefits that a sponsor in the 1970s would not get. Prudential paid ₹18 lakh to get naming rights for the 1975 World Cup. Even taking out all the extra goodies a sponsor gets today, the factor of increase would be about over 100 times a title sponsor in the 1970s. With these kind of sponsorship rights the sponsorship ceases to be part of the marketing strategy, it is, in fact, the all consuming marketing obsession in that year of sponsorship.[1]

The technical reason for the wider application of sponsorships is the 'activation ratio'. The ratio of exploitation (or spend on media, events and promotions with the sponsorship in it) to sponsorship rights should be a multiple, not a fraction. To explain this further, if you spend ₹10 crore in getting the right to say 'Official Sponsor of Property X' you should be in a position to spend atleast three times as much or ₹30 crore on TV advertising, promotion and events using the sponsorship asset (Property X). One way of doing this is to buy an asset that can be used in many countries.

Bigger deals when allocated across countries have a better activation ratio than many individual mid-size deals across many countries.

Global or regional tournament sponsorship is another manifestation of global alliances in sport. Just as there are winners taking all in sport, there are winners taking all in media. The cost of bidding for media rights for a sporting event is so prohibitively high that just a few players can come to the table. Complexities of language have been resolved with technology, which permits split beams of the same event to be broadcast in different languages by the same channel. Thus, a music event can be broadcast by MTV simultaneously in Thailand, Malaysia and Singapore, and you can advertise your choice of brand and language in all these countries.

[1] *Live Mint* for Vodafone Essar data, cricinfo.com for 1975 Prudential Cup data.

USING CRICKET TO BUILD OTHER SPORTS

Carlsberg, one of the sponsors of the football Euro 2008, roped in cricketer Yuvraj Singh to attend an event to build the Carlsberg brand in India. We don't know how much this helped the Carlsberg brand, but it shows the extent to which sports marketing in India is linked to cricket. Even Vodafone made Lewis Hamilton play the obligatory cricket match in India!

Reliance has done a significant job of building on their cricketing credentials (after all they were a World Cup title sponsor and are now owners of the Mumbai Indians in the IPL) to build other sports. In March 2010 they started a joint venture with IMG (International Management Group), the sports management company. In June 2010 they signed up the Basketball federation of India for the rights to basketball for the next thirty years. Then IMG–Reliance signed a $155 million (₹70 crore) deal with the All India Football Federation giving it all commercial rights in football (9 December 2010). They are 'taking a position' in sports other than cricket with these long-term deals. We could be seeing the emergence of Reliance as a sports marketing giant.

More Indians are watching international football. There were different estimates for viewership of the English Premier League (EPL) in India – from 33 million (TAM Sports) to 62 million (*The Guardian*, 25 July 2008) in 2008. This is respectable but still small in comparison with the 143 million viewers that IPL 3 managed to get, which means the EPL is catching on but slowly.

This probably means that we shall see EPL football teams and stars coming to India in the foreseeable future. This is the 'formula' football franchisees have used to build a loyal fan base in Southeast Asia.

Recently I (Shyam) visited the historic Maracana stadium in Rio de Janeiro, officially called the Estádio Jornalista Mário Filho. It is a part of Brazil's cultural heritage, having hosted many great players. It is also where Brazil lost the World Cup final, 1–2, to Uruguay in 1950. It is a storehouse of football memorabilia, with wonderful photographs of players, past and present, juxtaposed on the walls, footmarks embedded in cement, and quotes by football greats. Some are more interesting than others. A quote dated 1921, by a Brazilian writer Graciliano Ramos is rather telling: 'Football will not catch on, you can be sure of it.'

At the cusp in India, history could repeat itself, and who knows – football could one day become a competitor to cricket. We may not play in world cups but we can definitely watch world cups as well as anyone else.

There are several reasons for our assertion. In the top six metropolises, TV viewership went up from 16.2 million for the 2006 FIFA World Cup to 32.6 million in the 2010 World Cup. Secondly, 25 per cent of the viewers in 2010 were in the 15–24 age group as opposed to 21 per cent in 2006. The advertising revenue generated in 2010 was ₹150 crore, as against ₹55 crore in 2006. Some estimates are more conservative, placing the 2010 revenues at ₹100 crore, which is still nearly double the figure for 2006. In contrast, while the cricket World Cup 2011 is expected to generate a revenue of ₹750 crore, the corresponding figure for IPL 4 in 2011 is ₹1000 crore!

Looking beyond the top six metros, 53 million people watched the 2010 Football World Cup, a significant number but still a small number as against the 143 million who watched IPL 3.[2]

[2] TAM Sports, AdEx.

WITH A BAT AND A MALL

Over time, small retail stores have been edged out by large malls. This is a global phenomenon and one that is now visible in most Indian cities. These malls target the middle- and upper-middle classes and a young demographic. Many stores in these malls have retail outlets of international brands and more often than not, they closely mirror the store's design and layout globally. Consumers who shop at these stores are likely to encounter visuals of Andy Roddick or Rafael Nadal, as they are both global brand ambassadors. Retail stores of international brands customize themselves according to the needs of a specific country (for instance Gillette's 'Men in black' campaign had Derek Jeter in the US, Thierry Henry in Europe and Rahul Dravid in India), but retain some of the visual imagery you would see in their stores in Singapore, Hong Kong or anywhere else in the world. Luxury brands, in particular, have a consistency to them, as their consumers are internationally mobile.

In summary, there are some very big trends that are driving the increasing salience of international sportspersons in India. The first is performance, the second, international events and media alliances and the third, the growing mall culture. None of these trends is likely to reverse in the years to come and so we will see more and not less of international sports marketing. The fact that the Indian consumer is open to international sportspersons as credible ambassadors is also a contributory factor to this.

While sports marketing has, without doubt, benefited some, but as it is in every game, here too, there have been losers. We will be covering the fall of hockey soon, but you can add specialist Test cricketers to the losers' list, as they get fewer sponsorships compared to ODI and T20 cricketers. And local sports like kabaddi, once the pride of the village, are now the collateral damage of the global village.

5

'Nothing Official About It'

The Cola Wars in India

In India cola brands and cricket have been closely connected over the decades. Cola brands have been endorsed by cricketers and have been major sponsors of many cricket One-day tournaments and Test series. In this chapter we delve into a classic case study focused on a crucial juncture in the cola wars over cricket in India. Although the 'action' happened in 1996, we will share the overall context of the Cola wars from earlier so the readers can understand and appreciate the build-up for this pivotal battle fully.

Coca Cola was a household name by the 1970s, when Pepsi was nowhere on the scene. In 1977 the new Indian government asked multinational companies (MNCs) to either reduce their shareholding to less than 50 per cent or get out of the country. Coca Cola, along with other companies such as IBM, chose to leave the country. In this protected market, a few local colas were launched, and 'Thums Up', owned by Parle's Chauhan brothers, gained a virtual monopoly in the market (handsomely beating brands like Campa Cola and Double Seven).

Thums Up had two memorable campaigns: one with the theme, '*Food, Friends and Thums Up*,' where famous cricketers were featured, and the second, '*Thums Up – Taste the Thunder!*' which still rings a bell even after all these years.

In 1990, the Indian government allowed multinational brands to enter the market on the condition that the brand name had to be partly 'Indianized'. Pepsi seized this opportunity and launched 'Lehar Pepsi' that year. In 1993, Coke returned to India with its original brand name; with big steps in economic liberalization starting from 1991, the government allowed multinational brands to be used without the 'Indianization' addendum. Pepsi also took advantage of the regulation change to drop its 'Lehar' addendum. In a surprising twist, the Chauhans sold their soft drink business, including Thums Up (along with Limca, Gold Spot etc.), to the Coca Cola Company. Once this acquisition was completed, most business and marketing experts thought that Coca Cola would slowly phase out Thums Up and position its own brand, Coke, for market share leadership.

Indeed, for some time, the company deliberately defocused Thums Up in its marketing efforts. But it soon realized that this was, in fact, helping Pepsi as without Thums Up, the Coca Cola Company was in danger of being left far behind Pepsi. In a case of eating humble pie, the company relaunched Thums Up with a new campaign that focused on reviving the mojo of the masculine positioning of the brand.

The competition between Coke and Thums Up on the one side versus Pepsi on the other was a war fought hard, and it is still going on. A senior manager in a cola firm once famously said, 'Our real competition in India is with tea, coffee and lime juice and only later against our rival.' While it was at least partly true, in the cola wars in India (as in the world) any marketing edge against the rival is vital. To be clear, marketing (in the broader sense) in the cola industry is not only about the battle for the consumers' mind space but more importantly, for bottling and distribution. Thanks to the Parle buy-out, Coca Cola had a clear lead on the latter (bottling, distribution and channel marketing), due to the large lead in terms of time (1977–1990). Therefore, for Pepsi to compete effectively, it had to get an edge in the consumers' mind.

Tapping Cricket and Bollywood

There were two specific arenas to fight for advantage in consumer and brand marketing in the cola market in India – sports marketing and endorsement by Bollywood stars. Coke and Pepsi played in both arenas. And winning in the arena of sports marketing in India is tantamount to winning in one sport – cricket.

Pepsi was smart to move fast on both these areas and what is more, decided to 'catch them young' – both because it is less expensive to sign up a player or an actor as a brand ambassador in the early stages of his or her career and because youth is the core target audience for the brand. Let's look at Pepsi's early brand endorsers: Juhi Chawla, Aamir Khan, Akshay Kumar and Aishwarya Rai in the period 1990–91. What fantastic bets Pepsi made! The Pepsi ad featuring Aamir Khan with Mahima Chaudhary and Aishwarya Rai, aired in 1990–91, is still remembered. Ironically, nearly all these stars crossed the fence to become better-known Coke endorsers. The same phenomenon (crossing over from one cola to another later) happened with cricketers too – for instance, Javagal Srinath. In Srinath's case, the matter went to court, but was settled later. In most cases, however, such crossing over to the other camp doesn't even warrant suing because the brand ambassador is free to move once the contract period is over.

Pepsi stormed ahead in the Bollywood sweepstakes by signing Shahrukh Khan in 1995–96. The Pepsi ad featuring Shahrukh with Kajol, Rani Mukherjee and Shahid Kapoor in

1995–96 is one that has stayed with many. Soon after, Coca Cola countered by signing Aamir Khan.

In the arena of cricket marketing, Pepsi signed Sachin Tendulkar, Vinod Kambli and Mohammad Azharuddin in 1993. Though Kambli faded away soon, Azhar continued to be important for Pepsi (though some of his brand building potential was wasted in ads featuring him and Jadeja in ridiculous situations, which we will elaborate on later in the chapter) till his lifetime ban in 2000. Pepsi was very smart to sign up Sachin too, early in his career.

Given Thums Up's intimate knowledge on marketing colas in India, the Coca Cola Company ought to have quickly understood the key drivers in winning this battle. Thums Up had carefully, and over time, built cricket marketing through endorsements by leading players like Sunil Gavaskar, Ravi Shastri and even great non-Indian players like Sir Vivian Richards, apart from sponsorship of cricket events. It was, after all, the cola leader. Perhaps Coca Cola was reluctant to embrace the brand itself and hence it was reluctant to replicate Parle's formula. A multinational company is often reluctant to acknowledge and adopt the success factors of the local brand or company which it has acquired. It is only now that MNCs are realizing the value of local insights, especially in the case of big markets like China and India.

Having reluctantly accepted the fact that Thums Up was important in the brand portfolio, Coca Cola accepted the importance of cricket marketing too. Once the company acknowledged to itself that a cricket-centric play was needed to win in India, it went for a quantum leap – it bid for the official sponsorship of the Cricket World Cup in 1996, with India as a key host (Pakistan and Sri Lanka being co-hosts). When Coca Cola won its bid and was awarded as the official soft drink of the event, the story of the cola war in India could have arguably ended, in favour of Coca Cola. Pepsi was facing its biggest marketing challenge – to find a place in the game, let alone win it.

Pepsi's counter-attack in this difficult (perhaps dire) situation is possibly one of the greatest sports marketing ideas we have seen. Pepsi signed many of the top cricket players from all over the world for endorsements and unleashed a brilliant campaign – '*Pepsi – nothing official about it*,' an appropriate reply to the 'official' soft drink of the World Cup. So powerful was this campaign that despite Coca Cola being the official brand of the most important cricket event of the decade, Pepsi emerged the winner. In fact, Coke was forced to limit its 'official' status image in media (because any reference to the word 'official' would gave free promotion to Pepsi's tagline!). Based on this experience, the ICC put in stricter guidelines on 'guerrilla' marketing, whereby a competitor of an 'official' brand approved by ICC is curtailed in its advertising just prior to and during the ICC event (like the World Cup), besides banning the use of the competing product in the stadium. Pepsi's campaign was a 'game changer' in marketing (and 'rule changer' for ICC!) and it was, undoubtedly, a turning point in the cola wars in India. Because of this campaign and Pepsi's relentless focus on top cricketers thereon, not many people remember that Coke sponsored cricket tournaments (for example, in Sharjah in 1998); most associate Pepsi, much more than Coke, with cricket.

As Anuja Chauhan, creative director at the advertising company J. Walter Thompson, who worked on the Pepsi account at the time, explains: 'When Pepsi came to India they invested in cricket. They signed Sachin, Azhar and Kambli and made some fun ads. Then Coke came to India. They latched on pretty quickly to the big advertising truth of the nineties, that in India, whichever brand owned cricket, owned the heart of the consumer. Coke decided to invest in cricket too and, with big bucks at their disposal, out-bid Pepsi for the World Cup rights. So then we had to defend our turf, protect what we'd spent a couple of years building.'

Also, it wasn't just Coke that summer that wanted to be officially associated with the event. Because the World Cup was happening in India, *everybody* wanted that official sponsor 'chhaap' (stamp). As Anuja puts it, 'Things got a little insane. There was an official underwear, an official chewing gum, and an official "gutka" – the works. The advertising mantra of Pepsi had always been – zag if the world is zigging. So we zagged. Everybody tom-tommed that they were official – and we tom-tommed that we weren't. So we stood out.'

Pepsi went on to build its campaign with an unwavering strategic intent of signing the top cricket players and film stars. The biggest of all, Sachin Tendulkar and Shahrukh Khan, starred in an ad together later. Other big players (for instance, Ganguly and Dravid) followed suit in endorsing Pepsi.

Thus, despite Pepsi's natural disadvantages versus Coca Cola in all the critical areas, it had made significant gains. Between 1993 and 1998, Coca Cola lost over 10 per cent share points while Pepsi gained handsomely from 23 per cent to 43 per cent.[1]

Post the 1996 World Cup, Coke started a campaign with the theme that it (Coke) lives, eats and drinks cricket. Rather than going its own way, Pepsi succumbed to the temptation to 'respond' and came out with an ad with Azhar and Jadeja. In this ad, the players were offered a cricket bat to eat; they refused and the ad closed with the players drinking Pepsi. Coca Cola retaliated via Thums Up with an ad in which monkeys were featured; the animals were eating the bat. The ad closed with the line, '*Don't be a bandar, taste the thunder*.'

[1] *India Today*, 4 May 1998.

Who started the tit-for-tat marketing in the cola wars in India is not important. For, ignoring your competitor's campaign is a valid (and often wise) move. Why do two big, famous marketing companies and brands spend millions on insipid marketing? We think this happens when rivals become self-indulgent and start aiming the ads towards each other rather than at the consumer.

Mercifully, both Coca Cola and Pepsi moved on to better marketing. Coca Cola replaced its 'monkey' advertisements on Thums Up with the Akshay Kumar campaign on the winning macho formula and Pepsi refocused on its memorable campaign, '*Yeh Dil Mange More*'. The Pepsi 'ask for more' campaign was a global idea in an 'Indianized' form. As Anuja Chauhan explains: '"*Yeh Dil Mange More*" came out of the global Pepsi baseline – "*Ask for more.*" But, of course, we Indianized it, and made it stand for the spirit of youth, of cockiness, of irreverence, of being the underdog challenger, someone who's never satisfied, who's always seeking that next high, be it material, romantic or spiritual.'

THE AGE FACTOR

In our view Pepsi has defined its target audience – youth as a demographic factor (for example, under thirty-five-year-olds) and not as a psychographic angle (which is in the mind of the consumer); in marketing terms, the important part of what is 'young' or 'old' is in the perception of the consumer, not the actual age.

For the cricket World Cup in 2007, Pepsi created a fresh ad campaign (and a special WC packaging) featuring most top players – veterans and youngsters. Unfortunately for them, and a billion other fans, India had a very poor run and an early exit from the series. In the aftermath of this disaster, the Indian cricket team had to undergo a metamorphosis. Two senior players, Rahul Dravid and Saurav Ganguly, were dropped from the One-day team. Sensing the consumer mood, Pepsi dropped Dravid and Ganguly as brand ambassadors. Both these players were in their mid-30s, and youth was Pepsi's core target audience. Marketing wise, it seemed the brand was doing all the right things, but its big blunder would come later in the year, when it decided to end the contract with Sachin Tendulkar to focus on younger players.[2]

Dravid and Ganguly are all-time Indian icons and they were, and still are, big names in the cricket world. But Sachin stands beyond them. Sachin is a player of a lifetime – when you have him as the brand ambassador you should err on dropping too late rather than too early. Clearly Pepsi's judgement was misplaced. Second, Sachin continued to play One-dayers, and though he decided not to play international Twenty20, he now captains an IPL team, Mumbai Indians. Third, he has achieved even more in the last four years, after Pepsi dropped him, than he had earlier – he scored the first-ever double century in an ODI; got the 'Man of the Series' title in IPL 2010; was the top scorer for India in the 2011 World Cup campaign; and enjoyed a terrific year is Tests with his 50th ton to boot. Fourth, while Sachin is also in his mid- to late-thirties, fans think of him as perpetually sixteen, because he debuted at that age and because he has not grown old in his game. And there is a fifth reason, a fundamental marketing issue.

Jim Jordan, an advertising guru delivered a seminal lecture many moons back on selling lines (or tag lines) titled, 'Power

[2] Interestingly, despite his age, Shahrukh Khan was retained as the brand ambassador and was dropped only in 2010, in his mid-forties. This just goes to show that physical age is not important, but that the perception of age in the mind of the consumer is. A cricketer at thirty-five is 'old' but a film star even at forty is still 'young' in the consumer's mind.

Copy'. The most fundamental point he made in the lecture was the idea of 'full truth' rather than 'half truth', terms coined by him. The brand should be the focus of the creative idea and encapsulated in the selling line – that is the half truth. But the other half, the better half, is the consumer. Without consumers, the brand will die. No matter how big, powerful or loved a brand is, if it ceases to be relevant, the consumers will just carry on with their lives – without the brand. Jordan shared many examples but we will repeat two and let Budweiser and Pepsi explain the point.

'This Bud is for you' is a half truth; '*For all you do*, this Bud is for you' is the full truth. 'Pepsi Generation' is a half truth; '*You are* in the Pepsi generation' is the full truth. As Jordan elaborated on the concept of youth, the '*You are*' part of the line is not based on physical age but on mindset. Pepsi India in 2007–08 forgot Jim Jordan's lecture and therefore had to suffer in terms of opportunity loss and more. They decided to drop Sachin because of his physical age as he turned thirty-five.

It was not just an opportunity loss, there seems more to come. Perhaps Pepsi's worst nightmare: Sachin wearing Coke's red rather than Pepsi's blue has become a reality. Recently, Coca Cola has signed Sachin as a brand ambassador. It is not clear whether he would endorse Coke, the cola brand, or be an ambassador only in corporate areas – for instance, in the Coca Cola-NDTV social initiative of improving sanitation facilities in schools, especially for girls. As the famous Hindi movie line goes, 'picture abhi baaki hai dost' and we may see more on this front.

Despite the Sachin blunder, Pepsi's sports marketing in India has had more hits than misses. From having to overcome many difficult marketing situations, it drove its business and market share to compete for leadership.

Turning a Full Circle

Currently Pepsi is continuing the twin strategy of top cricketers on the one hand and young Bollywood stars – Ranbir Kapoor (with the 'Youngistaan' idea) on the other. For World Cup 2011, they came out with a fantastic campaign, '*Change the Game*', starring Dhoni, Sehwag and Harbhajan and based on great cricketing insights – Dhoni on his 'helicopter shot', Sehwag on his 'upper cut' (used as 'upar cut' in the ad) and Harbhajan on his 'doosra' ball. In the Sehwag ad, Ranbir is featured too, thus combining the power of cricketers and Bollywood stars as they did in the '90s – with Sachin and Shahrukh. With this campaign, Pepsi turned a full circle – from its 'unofficial' status in the 1996 World Cup to being an official sponsor of the 2011 version, but it retained its irreverent attitude.

On Coca Cola's part, the Akshay Kumar Thums Up campaign has been consistent. On Coke, they created a brilliant campaign (with many executions) with Aamir Khan over the years; and recently, they also started a new campaign, '*Open happiness*', with actor Imran Khan as well as non-celebrities. Suffice to say, both the companies have matured. Both feature Bollywood stars but on cricket and players, Pepsi rules the roost. At this point, both companies are arguing as to who is the market leader using different measures – retail audit and household panel. However, what is crystal clear is that Pepsi's 'Nothing Official' campaign and the consistent follow-up with cricket-focused marketing has been its big win. That 1996 campaign is an eloquent evidence of the power of sports marketing.

In fact, Pepsi's story doesn't end with data and business results. It has been further expanded recently to art (first as a highly successful novel, *The Zoya Factor* and then as a movie to come) – the ultimate success when a brand becomes part of daily lives and the culture of a nation. Although the novel doesn't name Pepsi, the author, Anuja Chauhan, who had worked on the Pepsi account, and the plot of the novel make it obvious.

In India, there is a 'love' triangle between cricket, Bollywood and cola brands, which is almost now a perpetual circle – each feeds off the other two. The IPL has cemented this relationship. We will come to that shortly. After an innings break.

6

Self Goal

The Fall of Hockey and the Rise of Cricket

There are a couple of serious misconceptions about sports marketing in India. The first is about the field of marketing itself – that it is just a gimmick, that it does not add value, and that it is built on lies. The second is that cricket has destroyed all the other sports, especially hockey. Nothing can be further from the truth.

In 1975, my (Vijay's) father took me to a stadium in Madurai to watch the World Cup-winning hockey team under Ajit Pal Singh play a friendly 'exhibition' match. As we waited, I had goosepimples while my dad excitedly described how great we were in hockey and how many Olympic gold medals we had won. The stadium was jampacked. This was not an isolated example of my relationship with hockey. I also vividly and fondly remember the commentary of India's matches in the early- to mid-1970s, in the voice of Jasdev Singh – 'Govinda-Philips-Ashok Kumar, Govinda-Ashok Kumar-Philip-Govinda… aur yeh goal!' The art of short passing in those days of Indian hockey was beyond language. Why would any sports lover not fall in love with such a game?

Alas, the magic and the excitement was not to last much longer. The decline of Indian hockey over the next few years became a harsh reality for all its fans. Barring the hollow victory in the Moscow Olympics in 1980 – where most of the strong hockey teams didn't play as the games were boycotted by many nations to protest the Soviet war in Afghanistan – we had precious little to celebrate between 1975 and 1982.

And then came the Asiad in New Delhi in 1982. As part of the rules and conditions of the Asian Games, the Indian government had to telecast the games in colour. A high-profile sports event sometimes forces passive governments to work. The advent of colour TV was a revolutionary new change. I was an engineering student at the University of Roorkee at the time, and in our college, the authorities generously replaced all the black-and-white TV sets on the campus with colour TV sets prior to Asiad '82. As a result, a section of the student body campaigned for the postponement of the exams – 'What was the point of having brand new colour TV sets when the exams clashed with Asiad '82?' went the argument. The authorities relented and the examination schedule was altered.

We all watched many events of Asiad '82 but the most eagerly awaited one was the hockey final – India vs. Pakistan. The occasion couldn't have been bigger or better. Never have I seen so many people gathered in one room to watch TV. All the good seats were taken well before the match. 'Floor seating' was cramped, without any safety precautions. Many sat on a narrow parapet, with their legs dangling in the air. How the parapet didn't collapse, I can't explain – perhaps this was proof of the strength of our civil engineering. From what we could see on TV of the National Stadium in Delhi, there was not a seat empty at the stadium either.

When India scored a goal, the cheering was beyond any I have experienced in my life. After all, it was the final, we were watching it in colour, and India had taken a lead against Pakistan – how much better could a hockey game get? And then, in a disaster of gigantic proportions, Pakistan mauled us 7–1. The silence in the room was deafening. We were too shocked to react at first. And then, the blame game began.

'This guy Negi has been bought,' someone claimed. 'It was rigged, man,' another consoled himself. 'Match fixing yaar,' shouted someone. Of course, all these comments were generously peppered with abuses, the accepted lingo in a boys' hostel.

Now, I have been scarred by Pakistani cricket players many times during my engineering days (1982–86) – there was the ending of the career of Viswanath, who could not tackle the ferocious bowling by Imran Khan and company in the Test series in Pakistan in 1982–83; and the last-ball six by Miandad off Chetan Sharma in Sharjah in 1986 when Pakistan needed four runs to win, among other humiliations. Over time, the scars have healed. But the scars of the Asiad '82 hockey debacle won't heal. Or so I thought until our win against Pakistan in the Commonwealth Games in 2010.

Interestingly, Negi's side of the story, unheard for a decade and a half, would find expression in *Chak De India*, the 2007 Bollywood blockbuster.

How TV Drove Passion for Cricket

In the sixties and the seventies, the Indian fan was used to the feats of the hockey team and a dismal show by the cricket team (barring some sterling performances, such as victories over the West Indies and England in 1971). But that was the radio era. The Asiad '82 hockey debacle – and India's unexpected cricket World Cup victory the following year – both watched by millions on TV, turned the tables. The image of Kapil Dev's million-watt smile and the jubilant Indian team holding the Cup stood in stark contrast to the 1982 Asiad hockey final, and perhaps that is what shifted my generation's passion from 'partially hockey' to 'fully cricket'. Mind you, the transition had nothing to do with money in cricket, or the power of the

BCCI or any other extraneous reason; it was one single but all-powerful factor – performance.

If we had had live TV coverage and millions of TV sets in the country in earlier decades and if we had watched the glorious hockey triumphs of earlier decades, then would our sports history been different?

As Shekhar Gupta, editor of *The Indian Express*, wrote in an article on 7 September 2002: 'It is easy to blame our callousness towards the national game on our cricket mania. But one of the greatest tragedies of our hockey is that its most glorious phase preceded the era of live television in India. Our last great championship victory, the Kuala Lumpur World Cup in 1975, was telecast live but then all of India had no more than a few thousand television sets, all black and white, and in the metros.'[1]

Personally, despite the 1982 debacle, I continued to be optimistic about Indian hockey. I remember one match against West Germany (as it was then) in the Champions Trophy in Perth in 1985 when we were trailing 1–5. Inspired by Pargat Singh and Mohammad Shahid, India scored four times, and sneaked in the fifth goal scored with only 20 seconds to go, thus drawing 5–5! This is the kind of hockey one can exchange cricket for. But it is very tough to remain enthusiastic for a team that suffers defeat after defeat.

It is interesting that despite the cricket World Cup win in 1983, we did not have live TV coverage of the first two India matches of the 1985 Benson & Hedges World Championship Cup in Australia. Doordarshan, in its wisdom, was betting against the team doing well, but it was wrong again. I hadn't fully understood all the hype about the TV coverage of Australian cricket and Kerry Packer. It was only after I

[1] http://www.bharatiyahockey.org/patrakaar/shekhargupta1.htm

watched the Channel 9 live coverage of the India-Australia match in 1985 that I realized how good it was – as different from Doordarshan as chalk and cheese. This was cricket at its exciting best, and India went on to win the Cup, beating Pakistan in the final! When the team arrived home, there was a live interview of captain Sunil Gavaskar. A journalist asked, 'People thought that the World Cup win in 1983 was a fluke. Does this win answer them?' Gavaskar, always a pro in front of the camera, said, 'Well, there are many sequels in movies nowadays – like *Jaws* and *Jaws II*. Let's call our win Fluke II!'

Thus, as Indian hockey continued to falter, Indian cricket rose. When the 1987 cricket World Cup was awarded to India and Pakistan, the fate of the two sports was sealed. And as for the next generation, a certain Sachin Ramesh Tendulkar on the field and the liberalization of the economy in 1991 made sure that ultimately performance would rule in the market.

OFFICIAL APATHY

Beyond the issue of performance, Indian hockey and cricket were plagued by the same shortcomings. The BCCI didn't like One-day games at all, in much the same fashion as the Indian Hockey Federation (IHF) refused to see the need to shift from grass to astro-turf. But with the wins in 1983 and 1985 and then the hosting of the 1987 World Cup, the BCCI got a whiff of the monetary possibilities. It is interesting to note that the BCCI was against Twenty20 too, perhaps worried about potential losses in its revenues from One-dayers. Indeed, India was the last major cricket team to play Twenty20. But once the team won the 2007 Twenty20 World Cup, the BCCI found love through money.

When Zee started its Indian Cricket League (ICL) in 2007, the BCCI, fearing that it might lose control over the game in India, approved the Indian Premier League (IPL) to start from 2008, an idea that had been on the back burner even before the ICL was launched. It is important to realize that both in the case of One-day cricket and Twenty20, it was performance (specifically wins in big tournaments) that drove money, not the other way around. While the BCCI, which is very capable of myopic thinking, was smart enough to capitalize on the possibilities, the IHF has been an unmitigated disaster over decades.

Shekhar Gupta, in the same article we referred to earlier, brings out the cricket-hockey divide eloquently when he writes: 'If hockey is the Indian sport's fairy tale gone wrong, Dhanraj Pillai must be its Cinderella. He made his debut in 1989, the same year as Sachin. Unlike in cricket, hockey does not so readily recognize individual brilliance.' I (Vijay) vividly remember how upset Pillai was (and rightly so) when there was no welcome for the team at the Bombay airport, when it returned from Bangkok after winning the 1998 Asiad, the first gold in sixteen years. 'I want my son to play cricket, not hockey,' he said. Again, this is the difference between the BCCI, which showers gifts on the players when they win big, and the IHF. For example, when India won the ICC World Twenty20 Cup in 2007, the BCCI organized a celebratory rally and each player was gifted ₹80 lakh. In contrast, the IHF could not even manage to give the players a well-deserved welcome at home; its reasoning was equally appalling: 'The team was supposed to arrive in Delhi but many players went to Bombay and no one knew that.'

Gupta concludes his article with the most apt point, 'Indian hockey's decline coincided with the arrival of live television and big sponsorship money. A sporting "product" was needed to sell those wares, to consume the sponsors' and the advertisers' money, and Indian hockey did not make the grade.

It had no Gavaskar, no Kapil Dev. And the basic principle of modern sport is, no stars, no cash.'

THE MARKETING CHECKMATE

What does chess have in common with marketing, competition, mathematics and philosophy? Emanuel Lasker, the world chess champion for twenty-seven long years, said something important in *Lasker's Manual of Chess* (1925): 'Lies and hypocrisy do not survive for long on the chessboard. The creative combination lies (sic) bare the presumption of a lie, while the merciless facts, culminating in a checkmate, contradict the hypocrite.'

We strongly submit that marketing is exactly the same. Lies and hypocrisy do not survive for long. If we claim something as part of the marketing campaign but the consumer doesn't agree based on his product experience, the brand will meet a checkmate in the market place.

In fact, we find chess and marketing quite analogous. You need to attack sometimes, defend at other times. Specifically, you need to fortify your position before you can defeat the opponent. Garry Kasparov, former world champion and rated by most as the greatest chess player in history, writes in his book *When Life Imitates Chess: Making the Right Moves – from the Board to the Boardroom*, about three key factors required to play for advantage in chess – position, material and time. You can 'sacrifice' material and still win as long as you have a great position and enough time. This is true in marketing as well. The branding gurus, Al Ries and Jack Trout, wrote a book titled *Marketing Warfare* inspired by *The Art of War*, a Chinese military treatise that was written by Sun Tzu in the sixth century BC. Given that chess and marketing (especially brand wars) are both inspired by warfare, it is no wonder that these two are analogous to each other.

Marketing is both a science and an art. Great marketing comes with a combination of hard work, organization and creativity. For now, we want to restrict ourselves to one aspect of marketing: the consumer, that is, the fan. As we wrote in our first book, *If Cricket Is a Religion, Sachin Is God*:

> ...in the absence of a fan base, the game of cricket would go the way of Indian hockey, a sport where the size of officialdom often exceeds the crowds in the stadium. To understand the game in all its aspects, it is important to understand those who watch it, even more than those who actually play it or make its rules. We identify two broad categories of fans. There are those who typically appreciate the long form of the game – the five-day, all-white clothing variety – who would applaud a good performance irrespective of the team, and seem to have an aesthetic attachment to the game. The Chepauk fan is an ideal example of this category of fans. Then there is the fanatic. For whom the event is a conflict between good and evil, to be won at any cost. The fanatics look upon it as a game about heroes and villains, with the heroes turning up for their team. The One-day Internationals target this audience. In this form of the game, it is significant that teams dress in different, more clannish forms of clothing.
>
> To summarize: Test cricket targets the fan, ODIs the fanatic.

We then go on to articulate how Twenty20, as a concept, does a better job of targeting the fanatic than the One-dayers.

To identify the core target audience, to construct focused marketing plans and to execute them brilliantly, are all important aspects of great marketing. We readily agree that we have seen examples of shoddy marketing, and some absurd and false claims, without any scientific basis or data. But to disparage the whole field of marketing would be the same as to conclude that all doctors are unprofessional because there are some rotten apples amongst them.

Under A.G. Lafley, the former CEO of Procter & Gamble, the company grew globally by 5 per cent in sales and 10 per cent in profits every year during his reign (2000–09), an achievement that is very rare in the consumer products industry for a large company. His first mantra was, 'The consumer is the boss.' This implies that in sports marketing, the fan is the boss. A.G. urged P&G employees to succeed with the consumers in the two 'moments of truth', as he called them. 'The first moment of truth' comes when the consumer picks the brand off the shelf, and 'the second moment of truth' is when the consumer has used the product. If the experience is disappointing, the consumer would simply switch to a different brand – at the least. Worse consequences could be negative word-of-mouth publicity, or legal suits. If the experience is great, the consumer will be loyal. Thus without the delivery of the promise that marketing makes, the brand will die sooner or later.

As Sam Balsara, the chairman and managing director of Madison World, told us, 'It is not that Indians love cricket, the game; it is that we love to win.' This is a very pertinent point. After all, if we really loved the game itself, then Test matches ought to be much more popular, and any great match – even if the Indian team was not involved – ought to be watched. Perhaps the IPL is popular because an Indian team (with a majority of Indian players) wins every match! In contrast, in the Champions League Twenty20 led by BCCI, supported by other country boards and approved by ICC (where the top Twenty20 league teams of India, Australia, New Zealand, Sri Lanka, South Africa, England and West Indies compete, similar to the UEFA Champions League in football), once all the three IPL teams failed to qualify for the semi-finals in 2009, the viewership was low, despite great cricket and the romantic run of Trinidad and Tobago to the final. And, importantly, a marketer wants to invest in winners, not losers. Though our cricket team loses from time to time (including a big loss in the 2007 World Cup), it wins frequently enough to sustain the fans' interest. On the other hand, our hockey team has been fairly consistent in losing.

An Opportunity Wasted

Hockey got a rare opportunity to rise from the ashes during the World Cup in Delhi in 2010. So many celebrities, including cricketers and Bollywood stars, were rooting for the Indian hockey team with TV ads sponsored by Hero Honda. The buzz on hockey was so big that the TRPs of initial matches of IPL-3 were affected. And, when we beat Pakistan 4–1 in the first match, the response easily beat any cricket news. As PTI said: 'The India-Pakistan match on the opening day of the hockey World Cup attracted record number of audience in the country, generating viewing figures akin to that of one-day cricket internationals.' Added an FIH media release: 'It gained an audience share of 8.9 on Doordarshan (TVR = 1.8) and 1.3 on Ten Sports.' (*Note:* TVR is the same as TRP, explained in detail in chapter 3).

The start to the hockey World Cup in 2010 was an excellent example of the power of good marketing and performance. But then, with defeat after defeat in subsequent matches in the tournament, the fans switched back to IPL. Brand gurus Al Ries and Jack Trout wrote in their famous book, *Positioning*: 'All brands have one chance; the leader has two.' Indian hockey has had two golden chances to reignite itself – the gold medal in the Asian Games in '98 and the great buzz about the hockey World Cup 2010 and its start with a win against Pakistan. Alas, it could not convert these chances the same way that it fails to convert penalty corners. Cricket, the leader, didn't even need a second chance.

We have stressed the importance of performance and delivery – the foundation of both sports and marketing. To be clear, the Indian cricket team has played badly too, from time to time. And its poor performance has had an adverse impact on interest and viewership – for example, the 2007 World Cup. But they returned soon after when India won a Test series in England after twenty-one years. Overall, the team has given fans a lot to cheer about in the last four years (2006–2010): winning Tests away – in the West Indies (2006), South Africa (2006), England (2007), Australia (2008), Sri Lanka (2008), New Zealand (2009); winning ODI finals (of the Commonwealth Bank series in Australia in 2008, Compaq Cup in Sri Lanka in 2009, Asia Cup in Sri Lanka in 2010), the Twenty20 World Cup in South Africa in 2007, and above all, the World Cup at home in 2011. On the other hand, hockey wins post-1980 can be written on the back of a postage stamp. The golden era of hockey is probably only in the memory of an earlier generation, for 65 per cent of the Indian population is below thirty-five. This young generation has never seen India win a major hockey title (barring the hollow Olympic gold in 1980).

In terms of global rankings, between 1982 and 2011, the Indian cricket team has achieved much. In One-dayers, the team is rated second in the ICC rankings. And, in the World Cup, it has reached the semi-final five times (1983, 1987, 1996, 2003 and 2011), going on to the final thrice, and winning twice in 1983 and 2011. In the ICC Championship Trophy, the Indian cricket team reached the semi-final three times (1998, 2000 and 2002), going on to the final twice, and finishing joint winner with Sri Lanka in 2002. Above all, the Test team is now #1 in the ICC rankings. In contrast, the Indian hockey team is ranked #9 in FIH rankings after the 2010 World Cup. And how many times has India reached the semi-final of the hockey World Cup or Olympics between 1982 and 2010? Zero.

Having won a silver medal in the Commonwealth Games in 2010, Indian hockey seems to have given its old fans a ray of hope. Except for the final where India were thrashed 0–8 by Australia, there was much to cheer for with a very good performance overall. Importantly, the ghosts of Asiad 1982 were exorcised with a fantastic 7–4 win over Pakistan in a crucial league game, which helped us enter the semi-final, where we came back strongly against England to level the game 3–3 and then held our nerve in the penalty shootout.

On a personal note, my five-year-old son watched these two matches live on TV with great interest and enthusiasm, wildly cheering every Indian goal. This was his initiation into hockey – a great start! Will my son witness a resurrection of Indian hockey? The eternal optimist in me says yes, but a more practical side to me, ruing the 0-8 mauling by Australia in the CWG final, yells a blaring no.

7

Dravid and Gillette

Consumer Marketing Vs Sports Marketing

Most marketing experts might agree with the statement that Procter & Gamble is the best marketing company in the world.

General Electric might agree, their CEO is a former P&G employee.

Microsoft might agree, their CEO is a former P&G employee.

Unilever might not agree, yet their CEO is a former P&G employee.

What makes P&G so great? First, its rich history and heritage: the company was founded in 1837; its first print ad (Ivory soap) was released in 1882; in 1887 P&G instituted a pioneering profit-sharing programme that gave employees an ownership stake in the company. Second, it has been a big innovator, having created many game-changers in marketing. In the first half of the twentieth century, when it was primarily a soap company, it sponsored operas on the radio. Hence the term 'soap operas'!

Over time, P&G developed many other consumer products in the market, literally creating some of them – for example, diapers with its 'Pampers' brand (launched in 1961). P&G also created the concept of brand management, an example followed by most other marketing companies. And in 1924, P&G became the first company to conduct deliberate, data-based market research with consumers. Lastly, it is the biggest 'Fast Moving Consumer Goods' (FMCG) company in the world – it has more brands with one billion dollars in annual revenue than any other company.

While P&G is a master at consumer marketing, we believe it has not fully understood sports marketing yet. In consumer marketing, the brand is centred around the product that the user buys and uses. In sports marketing, it is mainly about the fan's experience of watching a match in the stadium or on TV and connecting such an experience to the brands that are being sponsored or advertised. When the connection between the sport experience and the brand is strong, then its sports marketing is effective and results in driving sales and brand equity; we will expand on this concept in detail in the next chapter on sporting insights. Another important difference: the user of a consumer product doesn't want any uncertainty in regard to the product's usage. In contrast, a sports fan knows that it is the uncertainty that makes the sport exciting. Suffice to say, we believe that P&G hasn't fully exploited the opportunities it has had in the arena of sports marketing. In fact, it has made some bloopers.

Let's take the highly visible example of Gillette, a P&G brand, and its use of iconic brand ambassadors. Signing up sports icons like Tiger Woods (who is now, owing to personal issues, no longer a brand ambassador) and Roger Federer seemed like a good idea for Gillette in 2007. Adding Thierry Henry to the list was, on paper, a great idea too, to cover the massive base of football fans. We respect the audacity of the Gillette TV ad, in which the three literally throw Mach-3 razors at the users and urge consumers to 'trade-up' to (the more premium and significantly better) Fusion. This is a great example of bold marketing. TV advertising, of course, is P&G's trump card as it is the biggest TV advertiser in the world, spending over $10 billion per year. Nobody does it better, consistently. Beyond TV, Gillette has been using its brand ambassadors well in several other marketing initiatives such as store displays, 'Point of Market Entry' programmes, customer promotions and online gaming.

An Error of Judgement

When P&G was adding an Indian cricketer to the already formidable list of Tiger Woods, Roger Federer and Thierry Henry to its Gillette portfolio in 2007, it left out the greatest cricketing icon ever, Sachin Tendulkar, and chose Rahul Dravid instead. Now Dravid is a great Test match cricketer and has been a fantastic ambassador for the game; so his was not a 'bad' choice. But choosing him over Sachin Tendulkar was an opportunity lost, an error of judgement on the part of P&G. Also, Gillette signed up Dravid for a couple of years in mid-2007, and the timing could not have been worse.

What did P&G and Gillette miss by not choosing Tendulkar? First, with a tagline like '*The best a man can get,*' it was probably more fitting for Gillette to have Tendulkar in the company of Woods and Federer. These three were sports icons beyond the game itself. While Dravid is more suited for his attributes of reliability, protection and defence, Tendulkar is the one Indian cricketer who comes closest to words like 'best', 'total' and 'complete'.

Second, Tendulkar's on-field achievements and list of records expanded, and his stature grew even more (if it was possible!) during the period of 2007–2009, the same period Gillette wanted to sign up an ambassador. Had P&G signed on Sachin, it could possibly have extended the tie-up with him beyond 2009, when Sachin went on an even higher plane.

Sadly for P&G, what actually happened was that Dravid decided to opt out of captaincy and was dropped from the One-day team in 2007. This is crucial because One-dayers generate significantly higher TRPs than Test matches. The typical TRP of a Test match is 2–3, a One-dayer is 4–5 and an IPL Twenty20 match is 5–6. As a result of Dravid being dropped from the One-day team, P&G had to take the Dravid-Gillette ad off. Then, in 2009, they started airing an old Mach-3 (non-Dravid) ad. In contrast, to give an idea of how much Gillette could have benefited by signing Sachin, let us see how the 'Sachin Factor' drove viewership itself during the last three years.

The Sachin Factor

Year	*Average TRP across Tests and One-dayers with Sachin Playing*	*Average TRP across Tests and One-dayers with Sachin Not Playing*
2008	3.6	1.8
2009	3.0	1.8
2010	3.9	1.3

Source: TAM Sports, a division of TAM Media Research

But there is a more fundamental problem with the way P&G approached the issue of choosing sports champions. Announcing Woods, Federer and Henry as brand ambassadors for Gillette on 4 February 2007, P&G said: 'Consistent with the programme values, these three ambassadors were selected not only for their sporting accomplishments, but also for their behaviour away from the game. They are as much champions in their personal lives as they are in their sports.' The announcement went on to give details of what the sportsmen had done or were doing beyond their fields.

Now when a company signs up three brand ambassadors (and later adds others such as Dravid and Derek Jeter [the baseball player, added to cater to the US market]), and it also vouches for their behaviour both on and off the field, then we submit that it is asking for trouble. While having a portfolio of brand endorsers – as P&G did – is better than having a single brand ambassador, as in the case of Nike Golf, which only had Tiger Woods, the issue, in our view, was P&G's counting on the players' good behaviour off the field.

A blog entry, titled *Curse of the Gillette Ad, Mach 2* by Robert Mackey on *The New York Times* news blog (8 December 2009) made for interesting reading.

The writer started with what he had written a year earlier about the possible 'curse of Gillette' based on Thierry Henry's knee injury, Tiger Woods's knee surgery that took him out of the game for a long period and Roger Federer's losses to Nadal through 2007–08, including a loss on grass. Of course, Mackey might not have known about Dravid's woes, that is, that he had been dropped from the One-day team.

While the blogger was being too harsh – curse or no curse, all the icons performed very well in 2009 – the point is that brand ambassadors are not infallible. Great sportsmen have great on-field achievements based on their strengths but it is unrealistic to assume that they would not have trying periods on the field or any human failings in their personal lives.

This was not the first time that P&G had made a sports marketing gaffe. P&G had signed fourteen-year-old tennis sensation Jennifer Capriati as a brand ambassador in 1990. 'Catch them young' is always a smart idea. So far, so good. But which brand did they use her for? Oil of Olay. Now Olay's brand benefit is younger looking skin, with the core consumer audience being mature women. What a marketing blunder it was to cast teenaged Capriati for Olay.

A Specialized Area

The point we are trying to drive home is this: even the best consumer marketing company may not get it right in the specific area of sports marketing, for it is a specialized area. While companies like P&G deeply understand the consumers, they are not at their best when it comes to understanding the technicalities of sport and the psychology of sports fans. Consumer marketing companies are immersed in consumers, and sports marketing companies, such as Nike and Adidas, in sport. The tools of qualitative research, quantitative analysis, advertising testing and sampling are great in predicting consumer preference in consumer products but are not precise in predicting player performance; a lot of intelligent guesses and instinct is needed in sports marketing and a deep immersion in sport itself helps make gut feeling more right than wrong. Hence, a great marketing company does not necessarily become a great sports marketing company.

As an aside, but relevant to the point, in all our years working at P&G, we had always thought of the consumer as a 'she' and when we moved to the automotive category (with men being the core target audience), it took some time and focused effort to adjust. Male sports fans are (generally) more forgiving of off-field indiscretions but not of on-field mistakes. We shall expand on this aspect in a later chapter (Chapter 11, 'When Heroes Fall').

Though P&G has been found wanting in its sports marketing skills, we have no doubt that it is only a matter of time before they master this field. There are two important reasons why we say this. First, the company learns quickly – for example, it learnt how to make effective ads when the world moved from print to radio to TV as the primary medium to advertise on. It has also learnt how to make effective web campaigns, such as the Old Spice 'Isaiah Mustafa' campaign in 2010, which grew the brand's sales by 55 per cent in three months as per mashable.com.

Second, its humility, as stressed on earlier in the book. In 1993, I (Vijay) attended an advertising training programme in Sydney. I remember the P&G global head of the advertising group saying, 'We don't claim to know it all. For example, we don't know what makes great bank or airlines ads. But, we learn. For example, we are learning how to make great ads in the beauty categories.' Within a decade of this, P&G became a real master at marketing beauty categories – with several hugely successful brands like Pantene, Olay, SK II etc.

In fact, we have started seeing P&G getting more focused about sports marketing. The company signed a multi-year, multimillion dollar deal with NFL (the US National Football League) in August 2009 and was the US sponsor of the Winter Olympics held in Vancouver in 2010.

At the Vancouver event, P&G focused on a highly successful idea, 'Proud Sponsor of Moms' and reportedly invested $15 million to be the sponsor of the US team. It got endorsements from sixteen US athletes, set up a house in the Olympic village for families, bore travel cost for the moms (of the athletes), and even persuaded NBC to provide footage of the moms celebrating the victories of their children for a commercial that aired during the closing ceremony. The results were outstanding as P&G's consumer favourability ratings jumped ten points and market shares of its participating brands grew. The company reportedly gained $100 million in revenue. In July 2010, P&G decided to become a global Olympics sponsor for a decade (till 2020) covering two summer and three winter games, reportedly at the investment of $150–200 million.

It was smart to focus on the moms, the target audience that P&G knows best. But the fact that it has expanded to embrace the male consumers/fans too (as evidenced by the

NFL sponsorship) shows the clear intent to play big with sports marketing. When P&G gets serious with a clear intent, it invariably wins big in the long-term.

So what makes a company great in sports marketing? What does immersion in sport mean? We believe that great sports marketing springs from true sports fans within the company, who understand the passion and technicalities of sport. Sports marketing is not just fun and games. It needs hard work, strategic and lateral thinking, meticulous planning and excellent execution. But above all, sports, as a subject, has to be in the DNA of the company, an integral part of its culture, web and warp of its fabric. You can't fake it. With sports marketing, you either get it or you don't.

We've seen an alternate view expressed by some advertising and marketing gurus in India that the use of celebrities is lazy marketing and that consumers will not buy a brand just because a sports celebrity is in it. It is true that the mere presence of a celebrity isn't enough. But the use of the appropriate sportsperson to drive the brand isn't 'lazy' and this alternate view is perhaps based on inappropriate examples of sports marketing. In contrast, there are good examples of the use of celebrities, as in the cases of Colgate Total and Pepsi. More on that in the next chapter.

8

Dhoni and His Bike…

…And Other Sporting Insights

Sports marketing is not celebrity marketing even though leading sportsmen are celebrities. Celebrity marketing uses the fame of the person to create credibility or aspirational appeal for the brand among consumers. Sports marketing uses the credibility of on-field performance to connect with fans. A simple litmus test is to see a campaign with a sportsperson and then to imagine that same campaign with a film star or a model. If the campaign works, it is celebrity advertising. If the campaign only works with a sportsperson, then it is sports marketing. For example, Siyaram's had a TV campaign with Dhoni in which he was seen in cars with paparazzi flashbulbs going off, on a beach with bikini-clad women walking by and in high-rise buildings. This is clearly celebrity advertising as he could have been replaced in the same advertisement by a model or film star. On the other hand, Pepsi's '*Dhoni ki padhai*' advertisement, where he is shown as not studying maths but bowlers' hands, team mates and pitches, is a true sports marketing execution. That campaign would have made no sense if a model had replaced Dhoni in it.

So while a sportsman can be used as a celebrity, sports marketing goes one level deeper, into the sport itself. In sports marketing there should ideally be an insight reflecting a deeper understanding of a player or a sport – an understanding that other fans would understand. The sports marketer uses such insights to tell fans that the brand understands them. For example, the former opener and now selector, Kris Srikkanth, would walk to square leg after almost every ball he played. The sporting insight was that Srikkanth had some extra energy over and above that demanded by batting. The energy drink Maltova used Srikkanth as brand ambassador; there was a good fit between the insight of Srikkanth having extra energy (as seen by his hyperactivity) and Maltova's promise of providing extra energy to the consumer.

Currently any form of sponsorship, gate money, advertising on sports media or a broader overlap between business and sport such as developing a sports franchise or marketing a tournament are seen as sports marketing.

However, companies such as Nike, Adidas and Puma have gone one step further. They are truly immersing themselves in fans the way a consumer goods company would immerse itself in its consumers. A consumer goods company does so through focus group discussions, one-on-one interviews and seeking responses to ideas for products. A sports marketing company listens to fans, coaches, players and commentators to truly understand what fans want from their products.

The Fan is the Epicentre

The epicentre of consumer marketing is the consumer; the epicentre of sports marketing is the fan. Fans are a subset of consumers; they are people who follow sport closely and are liable to make their purchase decisions based on what they see as they watch their sport. This is truly where the 'marketing' in sports marketing matters – in understanding deeply the overlap between sport and the target consumer (fan) and developing products or offers against identified needs or insights in this area, and then commercializing them.

Sports marketing is relevant when a large chunk of your target audience is that of sports fans whom you can target in a relevant way through meeting sporting needs and through sporting insights. A fan's sporting needs can be very simple, such as statistics. Thus cricinfo.com developed a tool called statsguru that fans can use to directly access data. A more complex need of fans was that of continuous excitement in a One-dayer. Fans were finding the middle overs in One-dayers, between overs fifteen and forty, boring. This led to the development of a completely new form of the game, Twenty20, where there were no middle overs.

Sporting insights are realities only a fan would appreciate – it separates the fan from the masses and makes him or her feel that a particular brand understands them. Suppose we give a product 99.94 marks out of hundred. A non-sports fan would interpret this as a very high score. But a cricket fan is likely to realize that we are referring to Bradman's average of 99.94 and that what we were actually saying was that this was the highest possible rating we could give on a scale of 100. The fan's understanding goes deeper because he understands that '99.94', is a special number representing the highest that has been achieved.

Sportsmen can be used in celebrity marketing, and that is where the distinctions between sports and celebrity marketing sometimes get blurred. One example of a cricketer being used successfully as a celebrity in the 1980s was Mansoor Ali Khan, the Nawab of Pataudi, in the Gwalior Suitings ads. Owing to his aristocratic background from Madhya Pradesh, he was a great fit with Grasim Gwalior Suitings and the advertisement showed him in a suit with a fortress in the background. Eventually, the campaign was extended to include his family members. One TV campaign with Pataudi and his wife Sharmila Tagore walking through hillsides, with the latter cuddling lambs, ran for several years in the 1980s. Grasim eventually moved on but the campaign left its impact. However, this was not a sports marketing campaign. It was pure celebrity marketing and targeted upper-income consumers using Pataudi's alter-ego of the Nawab, as opposed to the cricketer. Had Gwalior shown Pataudi the cricket captain changing into his Gwalior suit after a game, that would have been closer to sports marketing as they would have associated 'captaincy' with 'leadership' and established the image of their brand as a leader. In this instance, as Gwalior wanted a premium aspirational image and as Pataudi was a Nawab married to a film star, it made sense to portray him as a celebrity.

Saurav Ganguly, unfortunately for him, is another cricketer whose contribution as a captain has not been reflected in any advertising. Ganguly has been associated with innumerable campaigns, ranging from Britannia Tiger biscuits (no doubt a link to the Bengal Tiger image) to West Bengal infotech (after all, he is West Bengal's 'Dada'). However, we have not seen any great advertising featuring him that is based on sporting insights, either as a turnaround leader or as someone with an eye for cricketing talent. After all, several of India's key players, such as Harbhajan Singh and Zaheer Khan, were handpicked by Saurav.

Here are some examples of how a company or brand connected with consumers through sporting needs and insights.

Need for Speed and the MRF Pace Academy

Indian cricket had for long suffered a sense of inadequacy as it lacked a genuine fast bowler or even a fast medium bowler. The arrival of Kapil Dev made a difference but still, there was a burning need for speed.

The fan understood the suffering, and nowhere was it felt more than when the Indian team got hammered by the opposition's tailenders. Indeed, Indian cricket fans have suffered from what we call the Tony Mann syndrome. The Australian leg-spinner Tony Mann played four Tests, averaged 23, but played an innings that had a bruising effect on Indian fans. Coming in as a night watchman, he was to score a century, thereby helping an Australian B-team successfully chase a high fourth innings score of 339 against India in 1977–78. (The A-team was playing at Kerry Packer's rebel World Series Cricket league, thereby excluding themselves from the Test series against India.) For some time after that, every tailender who hung on for a respectable period against India was branded a Tony Mann.

In addition, there was the phenomenon of batsmen who would do especially well against India. One example was the Pakistani great Zaheer Abbas, who was especially devastating against India.

Finally, there was the repeated occurrence of teams being able to prepare green tops and bouncing out the Indian batting, with no fear of reciprocal damage. At Sabina Park in 1975–76, Clive Lloyd was able to unleash Michael Holding, who literally 'let slip' more than a few beamers, and the Indian team was left frustrated by its inability to fight fire with fire.

It is inevitable that certain batsmen will do better against some teams. But with India, there was a more fundamental problem.

If a batsman happened to be a good player of spin but suspect against pace, chances were that India would be his team of choice to play against. Tailenders historically have been known to dislike the short, fast ball. On the other hand, they are generally happier against spin unless the spinner is called Warne or Murali.

It's that basic.

Ravi Mammen, the younger son of Mammen Mapillai, founder of MRF, understood Indian cricket and surmised that the solution to this problem was not going to come from inside the system but from outside it. Thus the MRF Pace Foundation was set up in Chennai in 1987 with Dennis Lillee, one of the greatest post-War fast bowlers of all time, as coach. There was something remarkable about this project. First, tyres are about delivering at high speeds, and so the project was in keeping with the MRF brand promise. Second, as a knowledgeable enthusiast, Ravi Mammen knew about this deep need of Indian fans, and also of the team, for a fast bowler. Putting together an academy to produce fast bowlers for India, with coaching talent from abroad, was a brilliant entrepreneurial solution.

The concept was brilliant, the staffing plan was visionary and was a story of true commitment and leadership. Ravi Mammen's project, funded by MRF, accomplished something cricket administration in India had been unable to do for sixty years – produce a steady stream of fast bowlers, thereby improving India's record, both at home and away. He will go down in history as not just a businessman but someone who solved India's fast bowling problem. Unfortunately, he died at the young age of thirty-nine, before seeing the fruits of his vision.

Today the MRF project has achieved far more than what it set out to do; it is now a coaching ground for fast bowlers from all over the world. The MRF project has delivered not only for India but also Sri Lanka (Chaminda Vaas, their most successful fast bowler ever, with 755 international wickets in Tests and One-dayers) and Australia (Mitchell Johnson, Brett Lee, Glenn McGrath). Virtually, the entire post-2000 pack – Zaheer Khan, Irfan Pathan, Sreesanth, Munaf Patel and R.P. Singh – are MRF graduates. In the 1990s, our two main fast bowlers, Srinath and Prasad, were products of the academy. MRF went beyond the pace academy by sponsoring the cricket bats of Sachin Tendulkar, Brian Lara and Steve Waugh simultaneously in the 1990s, showing their deep understanding of where the fans' eyeballs were likely to be focused. Twenty-four years after it was set up, Ravi Mammen's vision has made MRF not just meet the fans' need for fast bowling but also propelled the company to number one among tyre manufacturers in India.

As argued earlier, great marketing comes from meeting consumer needs and having great insights. Since the execution of the strategy is as important as the strategy itself, the MRF project must count as one of the best examples of sports marketing from conception to implementation. It impacted not only people's perception of the brand, but also changed the game fundamentally, by making India a training ground for pace bowlers. MRF, being a local company, did not have the resources of a Coke or Pepsi. But with targeted investment based on deep sports marketing insights, their investments worked more efficiently than mass advertising.

THE INFORMATION SEEKING FAN AND *CRICKET WITH VIJAY MERCHANT*

Now to write about a marketing programme that was built on a deep sporting insight.

Before Gavaskar there was another Bombay opener, one with a higher first class average (71), who also used sports marketing insightfully for his business. We are referring to Vijay Merchant, the compact Indian opener, captain, administrator, selector and businessman. Merchant, who belonged to the affluent, mill-owning Thackersey family, was actually named Vijay Thackersey, but owing to the inability of his English school principal to decipher his surname, it was simplified to Merchant.

Merchant was an interesting figure. He could hook the ball (very rare for a Bombay batsman of that vintage); his rivalry with Vijay Hazare was legendary; and his bold decisions as selector, such as bringing back leg-spinner Chandrasekhar, led to that golden phase in 1971 when India won an away series in England for the first time.

Merchant is reported to have said that he played cricket with a straight bat, and life, which was on a more treacherous wicket, with a cross bat, but neither with a crooked bat.

Marketing Merchant

Merchant created a radio chat show called *Cricket with Vijay Merchant*, which became a Sunday afternoon ritual for many cricket fans. He would comment on the current cricket season, the performance of the Indian team and of individual players, and more than occasionally, talk about the great players of the past.

I wrote to Vijay Merchant once, complaining that fast bowlers routinely left the field in between their spells and asked him why umpires did not insist on their staying out of the field of play for as long as their 'unofficial break'. I was surprised and delighted to receive a response from the great man and an invitation for tea. I reached a meeting room in Colaba where other letter writers had been invited. I found a group of regulars. Merchant would address their queries and also give suggestions. In reply to my question, he said the umpires had the discretion to decide whether the spirit of the game was being violated or not. They tended to show leniency as the subcontinental weather was not friendly to fast bowlers. One of the guests, an aspiring fast bowler with no contacts, was promised a contact, date and trial by Merchant on the spot. Merchant's radio show was an impressive and gracious display of understanding the fans' need for information and of providing a product to meet that need. Thackerseys' sponsorship of the programme made them a part of the fabric of Indian family life.

Mahendra Singh Dhoni and TVS

If Kapil Dev was riding BSA SLR bicycles (borrowed from a girl) to catch his flight in the 1980s, in the twenty-first century Mahendra Singh Dhoni was driving the more contemporary equivalent for two-wheelers in India – motorbikes.

The first vehicle for Indians in small towns is often a motorbike, and many of the consumers happen to be cricket fans. There is thus a need for a sporty bike, one that will accelerate off at the traffic light just as M.S. Dhoni is known for his sudden acceleration as a batsman.

Cynical cricket fans may sometimes complain that Dhoni's strike rate as a batsman has gone down after assuming captaincy, but Dhoni is that rarest of things in Indian cricket – a middle-order finisher. As the tension rises, the bat must weigh a ton. Goran Ivanisevic is known to have commented on how the racquet feels 'fifty pounds heavy' when you are serving in a Wimbledon final. More importantly, the arm starts to feel weak. At such pressure points in a cricket game, the delicate placers of the ball, or the elegant stylists, tend to hit the ball straight to the field, eventually ending up skying a feeble catch. What is required is someone with a clear, uncluttered mind who can lift the heavy bat, clobber the ball over the field if the gap cannot be found, and accelerate between the wickets to steal that extra run from the tiring fielders. M.S. Dhoni, like Kapil Dev in the past and, to be fair, like Yuvraj Singh, can do just that.

Dhoni's association with TVS motorcycles thus makes complete sense to a fan.

Many Indian cricket fans know that bikes are almost a currency for MSD. After his 2008 IPL deal, in an interview with NDTV, he said he had now earned enough to buy one thousand motorcyles.

Only a fanatic biker would go to the Lalbazar headquarters of the Kolkata police in his spare time to inspect vintage bikes as MSD is reported to have done in April 2010.

Only a fanatic biker would reward himself for winning a Twenty20 World Cup with a Harley.

Only a fanatic biker would own twenty-three motorcycles.

Having the hard-hitting Dhoni pose with a new sporty bike achieves two things: he embodies the brand benefit of power, with the fan insight that this is a sports person who truly loves bikes. TVS, which had signed up Dhoni in 2005, reported in January 2010 that its motorcycle sales were up 24 per cent.

Dhoni endorses about twenty brands, many of which would fall under the category of celebrity marketing. However, we believe an opportunity is being missed by sports marketers as there are plenty of cricketing dimensions to Dhoni – for example as keeper and middle-order finisher and as captain – that are yet to be exploited.

9

The Zoya Effect

How Women Got Hooked to Cricket

Sports marketing faces one in-built hurdle. The most popular sports are played by men. The fan base of most country and club teams largely, though not always, consists of men. Sports viewership too is rather testosterone-driven. Yet when it comes to purchasing, the decision-makers in most cases are women. Sports marketing thus misses out on more than half the consumer purchase decisions.

There are two major growth opportunities for sports marketing. One is, of course, its potential reach in emerging markets; the other is expanding the share of women viewers of TV and sports events.

This chapter deals with how cricket has systematically increased viewership among women, to the extent of changing the way the game is presented. We call this the 'Zoya Effect', after the book *The Zoya Factor* by Anuja Chauhan, which extended the appeal of cricket to the world of chick-lit.

There were three main developments that turned cricket into family viewing.

The first development was the emergence of the cricketer as a pin-up.

This started in the 1960s, with heartthrobs like Jaisimha, Durrani and Pataudi, who were known for their style and aristocratic demeanour. The trend got a fillip in the 1980s, with the rise of the dashing all-rounders – Kapil Dev, Imran

Khan, Ian Botham, among others – who brought to the game a rugged masculinity. It did not hurt that some of them were frequently featured in film and lifestyle magazines with various actresses and models, sufficient to turn them into pin-up boys in hostel rooms.

In the late 1980s, these players became the faces of products where the purchase decision-makers were females, products such as Boost (Kapil Dev) and Cinthol soap (Imran Khan).

Brands like Boost or Cinthol could have gone with models or film stars but the fact that they went with cricketers not only demonstrated that cricket stars could reach the eighteen-to-fifty-four-year-old female purchase decision-maker in a credible way, but that they could also drive sales. The emergence of cricketers as pin-up stars also meant that further down the road, a commercial starring a cricketer would not need to have a sporting context. Dhoni became perfectly interchangeable with actor John Abraham when it came to a motorbike ad. This meant that the cricketer had made the transition from being a sportsperson to being a model.

The appeal of real superstars cuts across any gender or age divides. Gavaskar, Kapil, Sachin or Dhoni don't just appeal to schoolboys looking for an autograph – they appeal to girls as much as boys, and moms as much as dads.

The second development that led to cricket lending itself to family viewing was the introduction of women commentators in cricket.

Cricket in India is at the same point as football is in the UK. The urban myth in the UK till very recently was that women hated football. With the rise of female commentators like Gabby Logan, and the ever increasing presence of footballers and their wives and girlfriends (WAGs) in newspapers and magazines, the number of women who watched football on television in the UK went up from 16 per cent in 2001 to 36 per cent in 2006 (TGI research). Similarly, in India, TAM India research shows that while Test cricket has a male bias (72 per cent male, 28 per cent female), the IPL, which is a post-2008 phenomenon, has a more balanced skew, with 64 per cent male and 36 per cent female viewers.

The Mandira Bedi Factor

Broadcasters understood that if they wanted to widen cricket viewership they had to alter the way the game was presented. This led to female sports anchors – Ruby Bhatia anchored the Champions Trophy in 2002 and Mandira Bedi anchored the cricket World Cup in 2003. Boria Majumdar wrote in October 2006 in *Outlook* that Mandira's show, *Extraa-Innings*, was a phenomenal success, getting 25–36 million viewers per show.

In our view this was the beginning of the Zoya effect, which was to transform cricket from being a boys' club into family entertainment. As cricket lovers, we are sometimes aghast with what passes off as media innovation, but as marketers we look at the numbers and have to admit that this was perhaps necessary to expand the game in the modern era.

TAM India's brilliant study, 'ICC World Cups – Myths and Realities' by Vinita Shah in 2011 clearly showed the increasing importance of the female target audience in cricket. According to the study, 22 million Indian women watched the 2003 World Cup. This grew to 38 million out of 105 million viewers in 2007. No wonder the brands advertised nearly doubled to 267 from 140 in 2003. The large female target audience makes it much more worthwhile for categories like foods to advertise on cricket.

Today news channels like NDTV and Aaj Tak and websites like cricinfo.com and cricketnext.com have female commentators and writers. Cricket media is, happily, no longer a male fortress.

The third big idea was building cricketing themes into women's content.

Why does a magazine like *Society* put Zaheer Khan on its cover? Why do film magazines targeting women write about tie-ups between starlets and cricketers?

This process of making cricket relevant for women has left no industry untouched. Not even publishing. One of the recent publishing innovations was *The Zoya Factor*, published by HarperCollins India and written by Anuja Chauhan, the creator of a number of path-breaking Pepsi campaigns mentioned earlier in the book. In this novel, the female protagonist, Zoya, is an advertising executive who becomes the lucky mascot of the Indian cricket team, and the hero of the book is the team's captain.

The book is significant from a sports marketing point of view because it integrates our first point of cricketer as pin-up, the second point of female viewership (in this case readership), and finally, also the third point, which is building cricketing themes into content for women. The book is now to be made into a film by Shahrukh Khan's Red Chillies Entertainment.

The book had a large initial print run because the chick-lit category is bigger than that of books on cricket. This is unsurprising. There is only so much a fan can read about dubious selections, dropped catches and self-aggrandizement. One of the interesting features of the book (from a cricketing perspective) was that it identified how important superstition could be for players. The female lead in the book was born at the moment India won the World Cup in 1983 (hence her relevance as a mascot for a World Cup campaign). The element of superstition in sport is a big insight. The twist in this book was that the woman was the lucky charm, not inanimate talismans like the red handkerchief (made famous by Mohinder Amarnath).

There are those who are less than amused by these developments, and we can understand their sentiments.

On 11 May 2010, in an article titled *Cricketainment Eh* in cricinfo.com, cricket writer and purist Gideon Haigh wrote that football and golf were not being subjected to the same corruption by entertainment (as cricket) as they were confident enough to stand alone on their intrinsic excellence.

But is this true?

Isn't football undergoing exactly the same change? Doesn't this sport too witness the endless display of WAGs and post-match parties, with TV channels covering lifestyle elements, apart from the use of stadium facilities for a number of events other than football and so on. Is the growth of street football, 7-a side, 5-a side, indoors football not a consequence of 'footballtainment'? These are new forms of football evolving out of the so-called degradation of the original sport, just as Twenty20 has evolved in cricket.

The reality of Indian cricket is that while it was saturated in terms of the male target audience, it retained the desire to grow. So it grew by changing the game, by adding new products like Twenty20 and by widening the target audience to include women – no different from what football has done. The male audience has reacted positively to these changes. After all, two-thirds of the IPL-3 final viewers as per TAM India were men. Test match viewers (like us) are a minority. The majority is simply lapping up the entertainment – cheerleaders and all. We are not going to judge whether this is good or bad, except to say it is a sign of our celeb-obsessed times. All sectors of society – the media, politics and certainly sports – have to adapt if they want to stay relevant. A sport like golf has not extended itself to the same degree that cricket and football have but that is also because of how well it has concealed its seamier side, which has only now come out in the open.

With people leading busy lives and with attention spans getting shorter, sport has to come in small, entertaining capsules or it will be replaced by something more engaging. Test cricket in the 1930s was competing with boredom; Twenty20 has to compete against the internet and the entertaining content on offer on websites such as YouTube. Those who oppose the phenomenon of entertainment coming into cricket must ask themselves whether they prefer the alternative – a world without cricket.

10

Going Global

Revving Up Away From Home

Sports teams are assessed on how well they perform away from home, as the opponents' home turf is seen as tougher to conquer. The same applies to businesses. Businesses that win both at home and in foreign markets are rated higher by people within their industry because they have proven they can adapt to different conditions. The globalization of sports marketing has opened up a huge opportunity for businesses to do well abroad. Even if a company does not have a deep understanding of consumers in a foreign market, it can still compete there if it has a deep understanding of sports and fans – as these feelings are universal in nature. An understanding of consumers is more difficult to translate across markets than an understanding of fans.

Indian Companies with Global Sponsorships

In the recent past, Indian companies have gone in for sponsorships of international sports properties like Formula 1 and the FIFA World Cup. There are good as well as bad reasons for this. The good reason is that through this route, a company finds international consumers or customers. The flip side is the 'arriviste phenomenon', where a recently arrived company seeks social currency in India by going in for a global sponsorship, even if it doesn't make much sense. One example is that of Satyam, before its takeover by Mahindra, going in for a World Cup sponsorship both as principal sponsor and as official services provider in infotech. This was an expensive way of building name recognition; after all, its competitors, such as Wipro and Infosys, had managed very well without investments like these.

Fortunately for Satyam, once it was taken over by Mahindras, its sponsorship of World Cup 2010 made more sense. Satyam had committed to a spend of ₹450 crore ($100 million) for two soccer World Cups, in 2010 and 2014 respectively. The perimeter boards around the stadium do get extensive global TV coverage, but Satyam's target audience was narrower – IT decision-makers in governments and corporates. And as the full extent of the Satyam scandal unfolded, it seemed to be a very expensive bet. Then the Mahindra Satyam entity was established, and the sponsorship made more sense, as Mahindra was trying to sell tractors abroad as well as computer services, and the sponsorship achieved the objective of building up both Mahindra and Satyam. Mahindra Satyam provided the logistics and IT support for the World Cup with 150 people on the ground; ticketing enquiries were redirected to Indian call centres. The use of Mahindra and Satyam in the branding was clever as it provided global name recognition to the entire Mahindra business. Mahindra Satyam now wants to provide logistical-IT support to more international sporting events. What better way to prove your product works than to place a $100 million bet (over eight years) on yourself? However, it remains to be seen whether Mahindra Satyam sticks with the original plan to sponsor the 2014 World Cup (as official IT services provider) or backs out. We have seen contradictory reports in the press, some suggesting they will back out others reconfirming they will stick with the original plan.

Meanwhile, Mahindra Satyam has also bid for official IT services sponsorship of the NBA, the 2016 Olympics and the 2014 Asian Games. It was the official IT services sponsor of the Commonwealth Games 2010. This is a case of sports marketing rehabilitating a company's brand image and exposing it to a new market, an achievement for which its leadership should get unconditional praise.

The United Breweries Group has invested the most in sports among Indian companies historically, with an estimated long term sponsorship commitment of over ₹1100 crore ($275 million). Of this $110 million is invested in Formula 1, and $111 million in the Bangalore Royal Challengers. The remainder covers Mohun Bagan and East Bengal (₹1.35 crore), other IPL teams (Deccan Chargers and Mumbai Indians), speed boating, golf and horse racing, among other sports.

Alcohol and tobacco companies have historically invested a lot in sports marketing because they cannot advertise in mainstream television and print media, and also because events such as Formula 1 create the kind of lifestyle imagery that tobacco and liquor are associated with.

To get around the ban on ads of their products, liquor and cigarette companies have two options. One is surrogate advertising, or creating dummy products that can be advertised as proxy for the main brand. McDowell's soda is an example. Another tool is the arena of sport, which has historically been more open to lifestyle products and less subject to advertising regulations.

Among other major Indian sponsors of international sports properties, Bharti Airtel is sponsoring Manchester United (May 2009) in a five-year deal for India, Sri Lanka and Seychelles. *The Telegraph*'s Mark Ogden reported in March 2010 that the deal was worth twelve million pounds. It is a bold move but whether it is a profitable one, only time will tell. Manchester United does not have the kind of following in India that it has in Thailand or Malaysia. (Manchester United's own research, according to *The Telegraph*, suggested that they have twenty million fans in India). But what Airtel is getting in return for its money is content (club alerts, player photos etc.) for mobile phones and access to games (kick-the-ball-into-the-goal type of mobile phone games). However, through this sponsorship, Airtel is also taking on the onerous responsibility of popularizing the club in India which is not its job. There are many barriers to creating a new sports market in a country – it is tougher than a new product launch – as we shall see shortly.

Bringing International Sports to India

Most countries are multi-sports oriented. The US has active fan participation and engagement in the NFL, Nascar, NBA, soccer and a variety of other athletic and Olympic sports. Establishing a new sport in this saturated environment is difficult. The UK is a similar case, with sports like football (soccer), cricket, rugby, motor racing, sailing, horse racing, snooker and darts, all having an avid following.

India is one of the unique cases in the world of being a single-sport country.

But there are some chinks in the cricket market, which sports marketers looking to create new sports platforms can exploit to their advantage. These are:

- The cricket market is large but expensive to enter
- There is too much coverage of the same team and the same personalities, leading to overexposure and saturation
- The cricketer is no longer seen as a hero but as a fallible mortal, especially with the tabloid culture now accompanying the sport

- There is the shadow of match-fixing scandals over the game

Within every category, be it a product, service or entertainment, there are those who like a mainstream brand and those who like an alternative product. If some people like Microsoft for its no-frills business functionality, others will swear by Apple for its 'cool' design. In entertainment, if a certain set of people like mainstream actors like Amitabh Bachchan or Shahrukh Khan, there will always be an alternative group that might prefer a Naseeruddin Shah or Om Puri. Then there are regional groups, which may prefer a Rajnikanth. Cricket's all-pervasiveness in itself creates a need for an alternative. However, it is not easy to create a sports fan, even for a globally popular sport like football, because certain fundamentals need to be established before this can happen.

New sports will need to catch people young, because they will then stay with them for life. Standing in a queue to watch a match with his father is a rite of passage for a boy. Then there is the peer group. It's a part of growing up to discuss the previous day's game with your friends.

All this has to be achieved before a new sports market for football can be created in India.

Then there are physical barriers.

Has excessive focus on cricket led to a less physically active population which is closed to any sport that makes them run for any length of time? Cricket is not a very physically demanding sport except for a fast bowler – and we have not produced too many genuine quicks. Arguments between children are usually about who will get to bat – not who will get to field or bowl. The idea of standing in the crease and swatting the ball around is more appealing than running from end to end of a football field.

In our view, cricketers who play other sports also are more athletic than those who restrict themselves to cricket. For instance, Australian cricketers, who play Aussie Rules football, and multi-sports cricketers like Botham and Compton were in their day, are more athletic.

New Zealand has a population roughly the size of Pune, but is able to put up a team that can take on the best in the world in several major sports, including rugby, sailing and cricket. Its record in motorsports and the Olympics is respectable as well. It has only one major football (soccer) team (that actually plays in Australia) and yet managed to hold Italy at the 2010 FIFA World Cup in South Africa. We as cricket fans have seen how a Craig McMillan or a Scott Styris is able to make up for his obvious deficiencies in technique with sheer physical strength and will power, all thanks to the number of sports each of them plays.

Athletic and demanding sports like football or basketball have no sporting tradition for reference in India. The only sport that does is hockey, which had the misfortune of having its best years when there was no live telecast, and its worst day (Asiad '82 finals) when there was. Then there are the occasional 'one-off' geniuses like Vishwanathan Anand, who have managed to win at the world stage for many years but are not significantly rewarded. A Sreesanth may be better recognized than an Abhinav Bindra, a Leander Paes, a Mahesh Bhupathi or a Saina Nehwal, which says it all about the omnipresence of cricket.

What will a sport like football need to do to establish itself in India with the young generation (the older generation has accepted it only in pockets in West Bengal, Goa and Kerala)?

Apart from participation in the sport at an early age, creating a family tradition and word-of-mouth publicity, youth marketing, specifically interschool and intercollege events and regional targeting, may be more efficient than going in for a national campaign.

To understand what it takes to build a sport, you need to understand what fans are currently into and how much they are attached to it.

Let us look at the types of sports fans to identify a path forward for any 'seller of sport other than cricket' in India.

A 'Fan Involvement Ladder' has been proposed by Rein, Kotler, Hamlin and Stoller in their book *High Visibility* (2006). This shows how fans are involved in differing degrees in a sport. We will explain our understanding of it using the Indian cricket fan as an example.

Except for the first group below, all enjoy the game; just the degree to which they are committed to it varies. In escalating order of devotion they are:

Indifferent: People who couldn't care less (they may just tune in for special occasions). Every mohalla will have one person who bemoans how much cricket is eating into working hours.

Eyeballs: These are the big talkers who watch the game on television or the web but do not go to the stadium to watch it. Their relationship with sports is media-dominated.

Wallets: These are the highly prized fans who pay money to travel to the venue and wait in interminable queues to watch games. They bring energy (and money) to the game.

Collectors: People who buy memorabilia and sports merchandise, like the ball with which Anil Kumble took ten wickets in an innings.

Groupies or Chamchas: Fans who want to meet cricketers. Think of the fan who will attend an IPL party with an attendance fee of ₹50,000, just to meet cricketers.

Insiders: Now we are talking serious investment. Fans who buy equity in teams or donate to sports scholarships. For instance, the owners of IPL club franchises.

Ensnared fans: For instance, Saurav Ganguly's fans in Kolkata, who would burn effigies and threaten to boycott games if he was not selected in the team.

The goal of sports marketers, needless to say, is to metamorphose the lukewarm or indifferent fan into an ensnared one.

The hope for new sports is in finding an entry point in this ladder in the form of the fan who is indifferent to cricket or is at the eyeball stage. The key to winning at the eyeball stage is to make the media experience of the new sport more interesting. For example, football coverage now shows the manager giving instructions to the players on the field so the fan can see how managers change tactics and how their players respond. This brings a whole new dimension to viewing football, an appreciation of the tactical side of the game, not just the physical prowess involved.

Ultimately, the football marketer has to make the Indian fan feel that the prospect of watching Lionel Messi is better than watching the Indian team field in a Twenty20 match, which seems highly unlikely.

For a normal sponsor, the real problem is the minimal return on investment. And so the question: Why should anyone invest in building a sport? Up until the 1980s, the cost of mainstream media was relatively cheap so a fan following could be built. Now with media costs at a few lakhs per 10 second slot, only a very committed sponsor with a very deep pocket can make this happen.

However, the global investment in football by the likes of Coke ensures that they will try to find a way to make football popular in emerging markets, including India. Presently, they get a better return on investment in Southeast Asia, where the game is already popular, where an infrastructure of stadia already exists, and where teams like Manchester United Football Club, West Ham United and Tottenham Hotspur Football Club are already available to tour to build their fan base.

The marketers of the English Premiership need to do a better job of marketing the league in India. The year-round action in the Premiership is in some ways more exciting than the World Cup as a spectator sport. Sometimes, when it comes to major events like the World Cup or the European Cup, all that some of the teams want to do is avoid losing, so they 'park the bus', that is, the entire team stands in front of its goal line, resulting in boring football. In fact, World Cup finals are usually uneventful matches because of both teams' desire to simply avoid defeat. Thus, the speed and drama of the Premiership, in our opinion, can be more engaging as a sporting spectacle than even a World Cup final.

To build football in India, the English Premiership, in association with some sponsors who are strategically invested in India, will have to bring teams and top players over to India and also find local partners willing to invest in a top class stadium infrastructure. This is the best possible scenario. Cricket needs some competition – the emergence of an alternative will improve the spectator experience.

When Heroes Fall

Brand Ambassadors Are Human

The word 'hero' first appeared in Greek mythology but the great epics all over the world are stories of heroes. The characteristics of heroes across cultures are common, including superhuman origins and strengths, a long search for something important, triumph over adversity, or a willingness to sacrifice personal comforts for the benefits of others.

Sports marketers who seek to make their brand a leader do so by engaging sportspersons who have the characteristics of heroes. In India, when a cricketer fails, the phrase 'hero to zero' is often used. But this is wrong. For on the bell curve of humanity the opposite of a hero is not a zero. The zero – or the average and the unsung – sits comfortably in the middle. The opposite end of the hero scale is the villain. In a world where warfare is now no longer glamourised, and politicians are discredited, the sportsman, unwittingly, finds himself filling in for the hero.

As brands look for leadership, they seek to cast themselves in heroic terms. It is an easy short cut. When cricketers win matches in impossible situations, chase down a big total, bowl long successful spells in the heat and sometimes sacrifice their wicket or break down with injury in the quest for victory, they fit the archetype of the hero and are celebrated. They fulfil the conditions of a heroic 'long search' for something important and 'triumph over adversity'.

The opposite is also true. That's why people who lose from winning situations are despised and tagged as chokers. That's why match-fixers are hated, because they have put their personal benefit above that of the team. They fulfil (equally unwittingly) the characteristics of the villain archetype. People do not throw stones or put a garland of chappals on mere zeroes, but they will go to that extreme only for those who they see as villains.

In sports marketing, there are several situations where the use of a sports ambassador with the intent of making your brand a leader can result in the opposite. We will look at some of these situations in the context of cricket and highlight those which we think pose the greatest risk.

What are the big issues in cricket which can – to differing degrees – hit a company's brand aspiration if it is using a cricketer as a brand ambassador?

1. **Match fixing**: Match-fixing scandals and cricket have been more than just good friends in the subcontinent.
2. **Injuries**: The constant grind of the circuit can result in physical injuries or mental breakdowns. If your sponsorship is with a fast bowler the risks are even greater, since subcontinental grounds seem to have been constructed with the intent of damaging the knees of fast bowlers.
3. **Embarrassing tabloid revelations**: Link-ups and break-ups with starlets, marital conflicts and photos of excessive partying.
4. **Substance abuse**: Use of performance enhancing drugs which can result in bans. Recreational drug or alcohol abuse is also a risk.
5. **Political or religious controversy**: The involvement of sportspersons in political or religious causes. It is a

recurring nightmare for a sponsor to have a player join a political party as that costs him or her half or more of the fan base immediately.

6. **Poor performance**: When a company signs up a player, it does so on the basis of the player's past performance. But there is no guarantee that the player will continue to sustain his or her form.
7. **Disreputable behaviour**: This can range from picking up a fight to being excessively rude with fans and the press, and being disruptive at public forums.

Let's look at these in more detail.

Match Fixing

To the male cricket fan in India, selling the team out to gamblers is a worse crime than a scandal in a player's personal life. For example, on 7 April 2000, the Delhi Police released wiretapes of the South African captain Hansie Cronje's conversations with a bookie, showing he was fixing events in the then ongoing India–South Africa ODI series. The ensuing investigation spread across the cricketing world, and also resulted in a ban on Azharuddin. Other players like Ajay Jadeja (whose ban was quashed by the Delhi High Court in 2003), Manoj Prabhakar and Ajay Sharma were cited as having links with bookies. Some of these players (Azhar and Jadeja) were quickly dropped from the Pepsi commercials.

Now we have seen cricketers tainted by the match-fixing scandal being resurrected as politicians or as media anchors. This is because politicians and media personalities are not expected to be heroes in the same way as sportspersons, who are not supposed to let their side down deliberately. The Indian fan is attached to his team to an irrational degree and will see match-fixing as a major issue. No person tainted by match-fixing in India has played for the country again, even if they have resurrected their careers elsewhere.

Bill Shankly, the Liverpool football coach, is quoted as having said, 'Football is not a matter of life and death. It's much more important than that.' For the Indian cricket fan, for whom cricket is more important than life or death, selling out the team is unacceptable.

Injuries

Heroes can fall in the pursuit of victory. In fact, an easy win is not heroic at all – it is anti-climactic.

In sport, an injury, especially on-field, is sometimes seen by fans as a red badge of courage. It implies that the player played so hard for the team that his body paid the price. It is consistent with the fans' perception of a sportsperson as a gladiatorial hero. When Kapil Dev had a knee operation in 1984, there was considerable fan sympathy for him as he was seen as having got the injury because he was overbowled. Mohinder Amarnath was a hero in the West Indies tour of 1982–83, despite India's loss, because he was willing to be hit by fast bowlers on the body rather than give his wicket away. A player who gets injured in the pursuit of team victory continues to have a great image, a better one at least than one who starts moving towards the square leg umpire at the sign of a fast bowler!

The impact of player injuries on a sponsor depends on how severe the injury is, how it was sustained and how long it would keep the player out of the game. If it's a short-term injury caused by events on the field, then it is not a risk. But if the injury is long term then the sponsor will have to think of terminating the sponsorship.

Embarrassing Tabloid Revelations

Fans are less excited by tabloid revelations as they neither confirm the player to be a hero nor a villain.

In the modern era, it is a truth universally acknowledged that a successful sportsman, in possession of a good fortune, must be on the brink of a tabloid scandal. And so it was with Tiger Woods. On 25 November 2009, *The National Enquirer* published an article on Tiger's multiple marital infidelities. In the month of December, his sponsors released a number of statements:

Gillette (P&G)

> 'As Tiger takes a break from the public eye, we will support his desire for privacy by limiting his role in our marketing program…'

AT&T

> 'We are ending our agreement with Tiger Woods and wish him well for the future… We support Tiger's decision and our thoughts are with him and his family.'

Accenture

> 'After careful consideration and analysis the company has determined that he is no longer the right representative for its advertising… We wish only the best for Tiger Woods and his family.'

Now contrast these statements with the one from Nike:

> 'He is the best golfer in the world and one of the greatest athletes of his era.'

This was followed up by a new TV commercial from Nike during his comeback game at the 2010 Masters Tournament at Augusta, Georgia, on 8 April.

Why was Nike's response so different from that of the other sponsors? It's because Nike is a sports marketing company that targets fans. It has a $ 650 million golfing line in which Tiger is not just a *part* of the marketing strategy, he *is* the Nike Golf marketing strategy.

The other brands are firms dealing in consumer goods, telecom and consulting respectively. P&G owns Gillette and most of its brands target mothers. If the target is female or the product in question is for children, then the call has to be very conservative. If you are selling cereal for kids and your squeaky-clean brand ambassador suddenly turns out to have a harem, run for cover because the moms aren't going to appreciate it. Accenture deals with senior multinational executives who are likely to be strict where values are concerned, and so Accenture had to be sensitive to them.

To male fans who are rabidly loyal to their team, tabloid revelations (like the concocted triangle with Yuvraj-Dhoni-Deepika in December 2007 or the PR story around starlet Lakshmi Rai and Dhoni in July 2009) do not necessarily indicate lower commitment to the sport or to the team. They are irrelevant. To people who are not fans, a tabloid scandal makes the player seem less real and heroic and more 'filmy'.

Substance Abuse

If a company's brand ambassador is found to use illegal substances to enhance on-field performance, then it implies that his or her performance was fake. By association, the company's brand will also be seen as fake. In addition the player will probably get a ban. In February 2003, Shane Warne had to drop out of the World Cup for using diuretics which he claimed he used for weight loss to get rid of a double chin, but which is a banned substance as it is also a masking agent for steroids. How did Shane Warne get away with it? The answer is that Shane Warne always gets away with it. He is a rebel and a rule breaker and has some kind of Teflon-coated immunity to scandals – fans are willing to overlook his many off-field indiscretions because of his incredible and enduring on-field performance.

Cricket is yet to have a major drug problem of the sort that has hit cycling and athletics. This is because cricket is a sport where speed and power cannot compensate for lack of skill. However, with injuries to players increasing and the need for power-hitters in Twenty20, this could emerge as the next big problem for cricket after match-fixing. One of the characteristics of a hero is the courage to overcome adversity, and taking performance-enhancing substances is definitely not heroic.

Political or Religious Controversy

Depending on the issue, a player's political or religious associations can enhance or destroy brand image. Let's consider the rebel tours by international cricketers to South Africa between 1982–1990. These players were induced by money to play in South Africa, where there was a ban on such tours because of that country's apartheid policy. To many of the players who went there, like Colin Croft, Sylvester Clarke, Lawrence Rowe, John Emburey and Derek Underwood it was a matter of job security. Others like David Gower and Viv Richards refused princely sums of money because they were against apartheid on principle. It simply became a question of willingness to sacrifice personal comforts for the benefit of others. An issue of heroism.

There has been no significant religious issue involving cricketers yet – and thank God for that.

Poor Performance

A large majority of Indian fans (and consumers) who watch cricket do so with the expectation that the home team will win. For earlier generations a Test match draw was like a win and a win was something rare and hugely valued. With the increase in limited overs games and the strengthening of the Indian team over the years the fan now has a sense of entitlement. When a player performs poorly, he is now subject to a lot of pressure from fans, and his advertisements are greeted with some derision. This also applies to teams. In the 2007 World Cup in the West Indies, India was eliminated at the group stage on 23 March at Port of Spain following a match against Sri Lanka. This triggered a massive response by enraged fans. Foxsports correspondent Ranjana Shukla reported on 19 March 2007 after India's loss to Bangladesh that a mob had stormed Dhoni's house which was under construction and destroyed some walls and pillars. Rabid fans had held mock funerals of players in Gujarat, UP, West Bengal and Rajasthan. There were threats on fansites to boycott all products featuring cricketers.

This caught sponsors off guard, and in panic they pulled off their advertising campaigns and cancelled their sponsorship deals. On 27 March 2007, the *Financial Express* reported that Sansui had lost ₹6 crore in pulling off an advertising campaign with Dravid, and Videocon had similarly cancelled a campaign with Dhoni. The Videocon chairman, V.N. Dhoot, was quoted as saying they would switch to film stars in advertisements after the cricket team's early elimination. Pepsi's campaign '*Ladoge to Jeetoge*' (If you fight, you will win) was another prominent casualty and advertisements to be broadcast with Sachin by Sunfeast biscuits and Pepsi were shelved and alternatives with Shahrukh Khan were used. If a business is now only as good as its last quarter earnings, a player is now as good as his performance in his last three innings. But marketers need to avoid knee-jerk responses to the fans' mood, which is very fickle. It's best to have a long-term brand association of the sort that Pataudi had with Gwalior suitings. But the media planners need to be flexible and buy more spots with the brand ambassador when the player is in form, and fewer or none when he is not playing well. Alternative creatives need to be available if the brand ambassador fails to perform. This is a better strategy to deal with the ups and downs of the game than stopping the sponsorship entirely.

Disreputable Behaviour

Sponsors should not sign up sportspersons who do not behave well in public fora with the media or fans, or in private with the company's employees. However, this is very easy to say and very hard to practice.

Ultimately, employee dignity and consumer loyalty are more important than the tactical choice of ambassador, for which there are many alternatives. The consumer is buying the company's products and bringing money into the company. He or she deserves to be treated with respect as do the company's employees. Yet there is a tendency to let superstars get away with boorish behaviour. At a media event at Kuala Lumpur, a well-known Formula 1 driver was asked by a pressman, 'What do you hate?' The driver replied, 'Events such as these.' This fell like a bomb on the assembly and the entire brand experience was ruined for all those present. Remember the archetype: a hero is supposed to put the team's interests ahead of his own.

Conclusion

Heroism in the age of celebrity has instant fame and riches as its upside, but also the downside of instant infamy. Andy Warhol once said that everyone will be famous for fifteen minutes. Perhaps in the future, everyone will be notorious for five minutes. That includes the sports ambassadors. Today's younger cricketers have been exposed to large sums of money and the good life far sooner than their predecessors, who had to slog it out for decades. The sportsperson is also a celebrity, and therefore seen by the media, especially the tabloids, as a legitimate target. Once a company decides to use a sportsperson to enhance its brand, it is simultaneously taking a risk that the move could backfire.

12

Indian Profit League

How It Grew So Big So Fast

Cricketing bureaucrats do not usually make headlines. In 2008, however, we could not get away from Lalit Modi. He was on television, on the internet, and in print. He was both the newsmaker and the news. One moment he was creating a cricket league with high profile businessmen and actors, the next he was putting up legendary cricketers on auction. He was announcing billion-dollar deals and moving with a speed unusual for any sporting association, especially the BCCI.

To understand the IPL it is necessary to understand Lalit Modi. He was a third-generation Modi, the owners of the Godfrey Phillips India cigarette empire. His life had been one of entitlement and privilege and yet he had a streak of rebellious independence. It is rare to find someone from an elite background who is a challenger to the status quo, but this is an important part of Modi's personality. He seems to be in his element when he is changing and challenging the status quo.

Modi's college years in the US (1983–86) were where he had his first set of business ideas. The club franchise system, the high-profile owners, the auction ('draft'), cheerleaders – all these were established ideas in the National Football League, Major League Baseball and the National Basketball Association. After studying sports management at Duke University in North

Carolina, he worked in Philip Morris in New York, which is a joint venture partner in Godfrey Phillips India, followed by another in Estee Lauder where he had his first exposure to the marketing of cosmetics. (Cosmetics were to be a big part of the IPL later!)

Rather than settling down to a comfortable life on the board of Godfrey Phillips, which he joined in 1992, and take the slow train to retirement, Modi on several challenges in business and this resulted in the creation of a four-billion-dollar franchise from which he himself has been banished.

In 1993 he led the modestly-named company, Modi Entertainment Network (MEN), which had ten-year rights to Disney programming. The deal soured.

In 1994 he signed a $975 million deal to get cable distribution rights to ESPN programming in India: the deal gave him India rights to cricket matches all over the world (except South Africa and Zimbabwe). In direct competition to media giants like Rupert Murdoch, he had seen a big media opportunity in India. MEN's job – to collect money from cable operators – was a tough one, and led to the creation of an enforcer image that has stuck with him. MEN also did a deal with Fashion TV, which is why you sometimes see Modi as a judge in beauty contests. Exposure to entities such as Fashion TV and Estee Lauder gave Modi some context on how to present a product in an aesthetic way. The relationship with Fashion TV saw a tense phase but was later resolved. Modi's relationships with business partners often resulted in litigation.

Modi grasped from the MEN experience that the business of cricket in India was on the cusp of explosive growth. So it is not surprising that his next step was into the murky world of cricketing administration.

He had a brief stint in the Himachal Pradesh Cricket Association in 1999 and later on in the Rajasthan Cricket

Association in 2005, both of which were political fiefdoms. In both cases he had initial success but was later eased out by politicians. A pattern was forming. Politics in India can be a good training ground for deal making and winning elections. Ironically, it is not a great place to learn governance, people skills or value-based institution building.

So how did Modi become so powerful in the BCCI? In 2005 Sharad Pawar took over as chairman of the BCCI from Jagmohan Dalmiya in a tightly contested election. Modi is believed to have helped swing votes in favour of Pawar in the election. Politicians like people who can win them elections. The BCCI likes people who can make them money, and Modi was to deliver on that front as well between 2005 and 2008, cementing his strength as the deal-maker in the BCCI. Let's look at some of the big deals he struck in this period:

- Team sponsorship deal for Team India with Sahara group for four years – $103 million (₹415 crore) in December 2005
- Team apparel sponsor deal for Team India with Nike for four years – $53 million (₹215 crore) in December 2005
- Media rights deal with Nimbus for four years – $612 million (₹2754 crore) in February 2006
- Media rights for overseas matches with Zee for four years – $219 million (₹286 crore) in April 2006
- BCCI sponsorship deal with WSG – $46 million (₹173 crore) in August 2007
- ESPN deal for Twenty20 global rights – $1 billion (₹4500 crore) in 2008

In 2008 he was on the cusp of his lifetime achievement, the IPL.

Modi's entire life (sports marketing, media, fashion, deal making, cricket administration) in hindsight was to equip him with the skills to create and run the IPL.

How did the IPL become so big? According to a brand valuation by consultants Brand Finance in March 2010, the IPL is worth ₹18,585 crore or $4.13 billion. However, we believe this is a gross overestimate and that the real figure would be around ₹3900 crore (see Prologue).

For a brand to get big so fast it has to fulfil some fundamental criteria. The brand concept must appeal. Following that, brand awareness, trial, distribution, performance (to ensure repeat purchase) are needed, supported by marketing spend and dynamic brand management.

Concept Appeal: The World Cup Kick-starter

Once the Twenty20 format gained acceptance, following the victory of a young Indian team in the inaugural World Twenty20 Cup in South Africa, the IPL was in effect preaching to the converted. Had India got knocked out early from the World Twenty20 Cup, the organizers would have had the dual task of selling the format and organizing the tournament simultaneously. The World Cup win ensured that what the organizers had to do in marketing terms was meet a need, not create one. It also helped that in one of the games, Yuvraj Singh, playing the tournament of his life, hit six sixes in an over. We asked Harsha Bhogle, commentator and writer, if he thought IPL would be a success when it was announced. 'I knew we were onto a good thing and that the league was overdue,' he said. 'But I had no idea it would be played out on this scale. The early days of the IPL, before the cricket was actually played, were a mixture of curiosity and awe… the kind of names that were being signed up, for example.' Sam Balsara, chairman and managing director of Madison World, told us: 'IPL is like "chaat" – sweet, salty, sour and, of course, spicy! Just as a food connoisseur would not rate chaat as his favourite food, the "purist" wouldn't rate IPL or Twenty20 as his favourite form of the game. But the masses have lapped up the IPL.'

COMPETITION: THE POWER OF RIVALRIES

Just as rivalry between Sunil Gavaskar and Kapil Dev expanded the sports market in India, it played an important role in the expansion of Twenty20 in India.

In 2007, Subhash Chandra, chairman of Zee Entertainment Enterprises, launched a breakaway Indian Cricket League (ICL) in order to avoid the painful and unpredictable process of having to bid for broadcasting rights of cricket matches. If this had not happened, there might have been no Indian Premier League.

Let us look at the chronology:

- The format for a Twenty20 league was ready and prepared by Lalit Modi and Andrew Wildblood, an executive of international sports marketing firm IMG (International Management Group) in 2006. Permission to execute this format was not granted by the BCCI for fear that the new concept would kill One-dayers.
- India won the inaugural World Twenty20 Cup in 2007, which sparked off huge interest in this format of the game in India.
- The ICL was launched in November 2007, funded by media tycoon Subhash Chandra. At this stage the BCCI was behind in the race.
- This prompted the BCCI to review their decision not to start a Twenty20 league (no doubt prodded by Modi).
- The BCCI then gave the go-ahead to IPL, which started in April 2008. The completed blueprint proved a good

> starting point. But what they also did was bring some of India's best entrepreneurs into the IPL as franchise owners. The collective muscle of these people would eventually win the day.

In effect, cricket moved from being a sport to a reality show made for TV. In reacting quickly to the ICL initiative through the IPL, the market expanded for Twenty20 cricket. The BCCI had access to the main cricket grounds in India, while the ICL had access only to the Tau Devi Lal Stadium in Panchkula, Chandigarh, the Devi Lal Stadium in Gurgaon and the Lal Bahadur Stadium in Hyderabad. In addition the IPL had most of the star Indian cricketers through BCCI contracts, and also the leading international players as the BCCI was a part of the mainstream (ICC) cricketing establishment. This control over grounds and stars gave it a competitive edge. The ICL lasted for two years between 2007–09 but it is possible that had there been no ICL there would have been no IPL.

Marketing: Individual Entrepreneurship

There is no doubt that Lalit Modi was a critical factor in IPL's success. He understood that the audience in India liked a gaudy, glitzy song and dance show, and that the Twenty20 format was about the length of a Hindi film. He guided the IPL through both the launch and the challenging second season in 2009, when the tournament was shifted to South Africa for security reasons. His ability to make quick decisions and move from Plan A to Plan B resulted in a smart, efficient operation. The clout he had obtained through the change from Dalmiya to Pawar, and the money he brought into the BCCI through the deals meant that Modi now had the influence to take decisions with speed even in a traditional sports administration body like the BCCI.

Powerful Franchise Owners

Some of the major advertisers in India like Kingfisher, Dabur and Reliance joined the IPL as team owners and so advertising and sponsorship revenues were guaranteed through the team owners. In addition they had management expertise (for example, the Ambanis, the Wadias, the Burmans etc.) and sports marketing experience (for example, Vijay Mallya).

Every business goes through a period where a risk-taker starts things off and then organized management comes in to consolidate and scale up. The IPL was no exception. In retrospect, had Modi voluntarily loosened his grip on the IPL and done less of the deal making directly, he would probably be still running it today. But it is hard for an entrepreneur to loosen his grip. As Bhogle puts it, 'We often talk about leaders as wartime generals or peacetime managers. Lalit was a wartime general and to be honest the product needed that. I believe a peacetime manager may not now be a bad idea.'

Media–Bollywood Join the Party

The presence of Bollywood in cricket is resented by many purists as perhaps changing the nature of cricket from competition to entertainment. However, the presence of names like Shahrukh Khan, Preity Zinta and Shilpa Shetty gave the tournament free PR through media. The IPL drama around the bids and the player auctions was based loosely on the US-based National Football League draft, which is a full-fledged media event in the US, in which thirty-two NFL teams bid for college players. The process generates media value and PR because it helps fans see their teams being constructed before their eyes; in other words, the outsiders become insiders for a short time. The fact that leading film stars were involved in the IPL gave it an Indian twist. Our estimate is that it generated at least 240 hours equivalent of TV coverage, because it was 'the story' for a month. In the process, the IPL also reached the female target audience, thereby expanding the market for cricket in India.

This would have made it the single biggest product launch in India, ever. With this kind of free media the IPL and the franchisees were saved the hard job of creating awareness, or putting their own money to create franchise acceptance.

The presence of Bollywood did one more thing for the IPL. It made the IPL an achievers' club, with the result that people paid lots of money to buy clubs. It was a status symbol, the new private island. This attracted a lot of very successful businessmen who for commercial and personal reasons needed to show their peers who the boss was in their hometown. Not everyone would have known at that stage whether the IPL would be a business success, but the presence of celebrities at least guaranteed a certain media value and status.

Product Performance Courtesy BCCI & ICC

The presence of players courtesy the BCCI and ICC also ensured product – in this case, player – performance. We have discussed the impact of the likes of Sachin Tendulkar on TRPs; access to the world's top players guaranteed a certain base media value on the basis of which the IPL could negotiate media rates aggressively. It is like selling a multistarrer versus selling an art film. Irrespective of the relative merits of the film, the presence of stars guarantees a first-day-first-show appeal. Further, while the BCCI had access to all the mainstream grounds, the ICL did not.

The most important game ever played in the IPL was not any of the finals of seasons one, two or three. It was the opening game, played between the Royal Challengers and

Kolkata Knight Riders. In this match, Brendon McCullum played the greatest innings in the IPL format ever, scoring 158 in just 73 balls. His innings, following a glitzy opening ceremony, put cricket back as the main show. The format had one match to prove itself as more than a gimmick, and it did. The probability of this happening was as low as Sachin scoring 200 in the first ODI ever played or Jim Laker taking nineteen wickets in the first Test in history. Nicholas Nassim Taleb has written in his book *The Black Swan* about events that are low on probability but high on negative impact. This was the reverse. A low probability event with a huge positive impact. In other words, this turned out to be a Golden Swan.

The rest, as they say, is history. The combination of concept appeal, product performance and wider audience (not just male) made IPL really big. As S. Venkatraghavan, former India captain and respected international umpire, told us in 2010, 'IPL has done a marvellous job for the game. There are eight cities/states now and there will be more next year. It has drawn crowds – even women and children who identify themselves with a particular team. So many people have told me that after six weeks of IPL they feel a void between 8 pm and 11 pm. During the IPL people could return from office and relax and watch the matches.'

Are Franchisees Making Money?

Though the IPL concept is a success, are the franchisees making any money?

On 18 December 2007 the BCCI issued a prospectus which described how franchisees would get revenues from the IPL.[1]

[1] http://www.espncricinfo.com/ipl/content/story/326200.html

The biggest item was television media, where the BCCI bait was a higher percentage of TV revenue to franchisees upfront so that they would reach breakeven faster. The prospectus laid out franchisee share like this:

- 80 per cent of the television revenue over the first two years
- 70 per cent in the third and fourth years
- 60 per cent between years five and ten
- 50 per cent from the eleventh year onwards

The other carrot the BCCI dangled was that of the central sponsorships like the IPL title rights (which eventually went to DLF).

Franchisees were to get 60 per cent of the sponsorship revenue during the first ten years, after which they would receive 50 per cent.

There was also a performance component:

- 80 per cent would be shared equally
- 20 per cent to go to the teams based on league performance (specifically semifinalists/ finalists/ winner)

The initial investors in IPL have reason to be pleased with their performance; their investment will probably fetch a 3:1 return if placed on the market today. Investors such as the Pune and Kochi franchisees paid $370 million and $333.3 million respectively with an almost zero chance of breakeven over the next ten years. This market has a logic of its own. The purchase of Chelsea Football Club by Roman Abramovich in June 2003, or Manchester City by Thaksin Shinawatra in July 2007, follows a similar pattern, leading one to conclude that 'goodwill' associated with owning a franchise in IPL is far in excess of any normal business.

There have been many complaints against the IPL – vulgarity, putting players like cattle on auction, dodgy deals, too much partying and so on.

In our view, many of the complaints are peripheral and for every criticism, there is an equally strong counterpoint. IPL has been a bonanza for many parties, particularly for the fans and the players. It has brought crowds back into the stadium. As Brett Lee, pace bowler for Australia and Kings XI Punjab, told us, 'IPL and Twenty20 cricket in general are helping to broaden the fan base around the world. From a player's perspective it is fantastic to play games in full stadia with an electric atmosphere.'

What we are concerned about is transparency, clean administration, and the fact that all matters need to be above board legally, ethically and morally. What is non-negotiable and beyond debate, irrespective of personal interpretation, is compliance with legal regulations of the country. You can't break the law.

Therefore it is absolutely right (in our minds) that the more responsible section of the media has been concerned mainly with this part – what is the source of income of the franchisees? Has any FEMA (Foreign Exchange Management Act, 1999) violation happened? Has there been any illegal betting? Has any 'match-fixing' occurred? Have any of the contracts been awarded with wrong motives? Has there been any breach of contract (with BCCI) regarding ownership and transfer of assets? In October 2010, BCCI scrapped the licenses of two IPL teams (Rajasthan Royals and Kings Punjab XI) for alleged violation of the franchisee agreement; but they are now back for the 2011 season due to a court stay. The BCCI also registered a case against Lalit Modi, accusing him of an alleged fraud of over $100 million. The Enforcement Directorate requested the foreign ministry to revoke Modi's passport, and this has been done.

There have also been allegations of FEMA violations regarding the 2009 IPL-2, specifically that money was transferred from South Africa to India in violation of FEMA. BCCI pleaded innocence, claiming that only Modi was involved in all these decisions. In return, Modi has declared that the BCCI (particularly BCCI secretary Srinivasan) was fully in the loop on the decisions.

More could be brewing. Most of these matters are subjudice so we would not want to comment on them. Our view on these matters is clear: whoever was involved in any wrongdoing (after a fair investigation), should be held accountable. Sports can't afford the integrity of on-field play being suspect. And as fans, we wish for early resolution of these so the game can go on in the field rather than in courts.

The IPL, in our view, is a brilliant concept and executed with excellence overall. Modi deserves credit for creating and executing the plan brilliantly. Yes, there are many flaws, which have to be corrected, but then Indian sports associations are never free of drama. Big money gets big attention, so it is extra important to be clean and transparent.

The IPL is still young. That such controversies have arisen now in its third year is a blessing in disguise. It is easier to cure a disease with early detection. As we wrote earlier, any wrongdoing needs to be punished – there is no other way.

The growth of sports marketing in India started with individual sportsmen like Gavaskar. Then it grew with the support of organizations like the BCCI especially during the Dalmiya and Modi years and businessmen like the IPL franchise owners. The next level, we hope, will be that of a professionally run organization that is not dependent on individuals.

On 15 January 2011 a seismic change happened in Indian domestic cricket. Rajasthan, formerly a minnow team, won the 2010–11 Ranji Trophy, beating Baroda in the final. The traditional domestic powers like Mumbai, Delhi and Karnataka did not even make it to the final. While Modi has been both lauded and vilified for the IPL, the work he did while in the Rajasthan Cricket Association in setting up the Rajasthan Cricket Academy (2006) and modernizing Jaipur's Sawai Man Singh Stadium (2005–06) saw some results. Ultimately the business of cricket will thrive only if the players provide attractive on-field performances and the stadia are worth visiting. It is this achievement which needs to be replicated in other states so that Indian cricket does not just have the richest league but one that can deliver a great cricketing experience to fans and high quality players to the game.

13

Rich Board, Poor Fan

How the BCCI Treats the Fans

We have articulated so far how sports marketing benefited many parties – players, umpires and commentators; the boards and state associations; sponsors, corporates and brands; media houses, and sports and news TV channels.

The cricket fan has seen a quantum improvement in his or her experience of the game: there is better stadia seating, much better TV coverage – with multiple camera angles, slow motion replays and the best commentators in the world on hand to interpret the game for us, a far cry from the dull, dark Doordarshan days. However, overall, there are still key deficiencies that come in the way of a fan's enjoyment of the game at the stadia; and on TV, we have seen with increasing alarm that the commercial aspects are intruding too much into the fan's experience of the game. If we had to blame one party for this excessive commercialization, it would have to be the BCCI.

I (Vijay) have vivid memories of going to 'Chepauk' to watch the India-Pakistan Test match in Madras in 1980. Those days, every alternate year or so, the BCCI used to organize a Test match in Madras coinciding with Pongal, the traditional Tamil festival. With associated festivals adjacent to the main day of Pongal and the weekend to boot, most of the days on which the Test was played were public holidays – a big invitation to go to the ground. And, if India won (as we did in 1980), most schools and colleges would declare an additional holiday to celebrate! So a Pongal Test was a rich tradition with a festive atmosphere; it was celebration of Test cricket itself.

Almost three decades later, I went to the MCG (Melbourne Cricket Ground) for the India–Australia Test in 2007. The Test started on 26 December, Boxing Day, as per tradition. There was a festive atmosphere (it was just a day after Christmas, after all), and tram after tram was filled with fans. It could have been Madras a fortnight later, I thought with nostalgia. But I realized that there were important differences between the Indian and Australian cricket boards. Cricket Australia always organizes a Test match that starts on Boxing Day in Melbourne; that is the tradition. Money is important but there are things more important than money and CA correctly understands that. In contrast, the last Pongal Test in Madras was held twenty-three years ago; that means that a whole generation has grown up without having experienced such a Test and perhaps does not even know what I am talking about.

My first complaint against the BCCI is that it has done its best to diminish the importance of Test cricket over the last two decades. While the number of Tests reduced in the 1990s, the BCCI gave us an overdose of One-dayers (as discussed earlier in the book). It also held Tests across the country (regardless of whether there were crowds for Test matches at a particular venue or not) thus making various state associations happy. For example, the stadium in Mohali is very good for One-dayers but the crowd for Test matches there is poor. The result: the day India won against Australia with one wicket in hand in 2010, most seats were empty. We need to understand that there is a rich tradition and heritage at certain Test cricket venues but not in others. Further, over the years, Test series at home have been limited to three matches in most cases, mainly to accommodate more One-dayers. Now that we are the number one in Test ranking, BCCI has suddenly rediscovered its love for Tests and understood their importance. In 2010 they organized, at short notice, a two-Test home series against Australia and South Africa each.

The second problem I have with the BCCI is that the facilities it provides at the stadia are still poor. In 2010, I travelled from Singapore to Mumbai to watch two IPL matches, including the final (as I had done in 2008 too). I had bought the best seat I could buy as a fan – the choice seats were reserved for players, sponsors and IPL officials. At the break (between the innings), when I went down for a bite, all the food had been consumed. I then had to settle for a snack of average quality later during the second innings. If the food situation was not satisfactory, the toilet facilities were awful, with only two of the four urinals in the men's toilet being relatively usable.

That the richest cricket board in the world cannot even provide clean toilets is a real shame. Even the West Indies, whose board is among the poorest, has better facilities at its stadia, as I saw in Barbados and St. Lucia. And the situation must be worse for women – I wonder if one reason we see more female fans at Twenty20 matches is because the match duration is shorter!

The worst experience I have ever had was in Mohali, during the World Cup 2011 India–Pakistan semi-final. There was utter chaos; I was in the queue for two hours and I was still the last! When I approached the cops for help, their answer was shocking, 'You also break the queue and get ahead.' At one point, I was worried about a stampede so I went away for a while. Food at the venue was totally inadequate. The toilet was dirty. It was mismanagement at its worst. Fortunately, the World Cup final in Mumbai was well managed with orderly queues, adequate food and relatively clean toilets.

Excessive Commercialization

My third complaint is the excessive commercialization of TV coverage. IPL's greed in this regard has crossed all limits – no part of a player's gear is left free of a brand name; an ad is always preferred to an action replay for the viewer; and nothing – not even the ground or the sight-screen – is sacrosanct.

But while I thought IPL was the worst in terms of TV watching experience, I turned out to be wrong.

The TV coverage of the India–South Africa Test and One-day series by Ten Cricket in December 2010–January 2011 was easily the worst experience I have had since the start of cable & satellite days – beating even the IPL! The first and the last deliveries of overs were blanked out more than once. For example, in India's first innings of the third Test of the series in Cape Town in early January, at a very interesting stage of the match and the series, Zaheer Khan had got out and with that, the Indian innings had ended. But we (viewers) didn't know that because there was an ad gracing the screen. Another big issue the viewer faced in the series was that replays of important moments were often shown a couple of overs later. But there was more to come from the Ten Cricket stables. For some years now, sports broadcasters have been using an irritating L-shaped TV cutout that features ads. But in this series, Ten Cricket went further. Even as the bowler was running up to bowl, a still commercial message suddenly popped up, distracting the viewer from watching the bowler and the ball. For the first time in my life I wondered if we were better off during Doordarshan days!

I have been a marketer for twenty years. I understand that ads fund the live telecast – that there is no 'free lunch' in life. I understand that channels need to recoup their investment. But there have to be limits. And I don't buy the argument that the channel is forced to do such things because the BCCI asks for too high a price. Let us understand a few important facts. Nimbus (a company that owns Neo sports and Neo Cricket) signed a deal with the BCCI for four years (from 2006) for the rights of all India matches at home at a cost of $612 million (₹2754 crore). Later, Nimbus managed to negotiate the amount down to $549 million (₹2471 crore). And, in January 2010, Nimbus and the BCCI signed a deal for the next four years at a cost of $436 million (₹1962 crore)[1]. Clearly, Nimbus understood that their original deal for 2006–10 was too unrealistic, and hence it requested reduction of the amount and got it, and then bid an even lower amount for 2010–2014, yet it still won the rights. It is also clear that the BCCI too understood the realities – hence the decreasing amounts. The proof of the pudding (why I believe Nimbus understands the value of decent coverage, making a bid while ensuring that it can make it viable for them) is in two parts: a) NeoCricket's (Nimbus's) coverage of the home series of 2010 against Australia was – though not ideal – better than the shocking coverage of the India–SA (away) series by Ten Cricket; and b) Nimbus gave an option so that the subscribers could go in for a separate high definition channel (at a price), distinct from the channel with the ads. On this high definition channel, one could enjoy uninterrupted telecast with complete commentary and zero ads in the India–Australia (home) Test series (via Tata Sky); I enjoyed this uninterrupted telecast on high definition channels of many of the World Cup 2011 matches covered by Star–ESPN (via Tata Sky). Ten Cricket did not give us the 'no ads but pay more' option in the India–SA series.

Ten Cricket's coverage angered many viewers – as was evident from Tweets and Facebook messages, written complaints and discussion in fora such as cricinfo. However, the onus is on

[1] http://www.espncricinfo.com/india/content/story/ 444304.html

the BCCI to ensure that such blatant commercialization be punished. In the first place, the BCCI contract should clearly articulate what the channel should ensure: that no action on the field is missed out; that there should be at least one replay of a wicket falling before any ad break, etc.

Recently Ten Cricket has been served a notice by the information and broadcasting ministry regarding the alleged violations of India's advertising codes during the recent India–South Africa series. The code stipulates that the advertisement should be easily distinguishable from, and not interfere with, the programme.[2] We are keenly awaiting the final conclusions on these notices.

It has become fashionable to blame everything bad in cricket now on Lalit Modi, just as he was praised for everything good in 2008–09. Sony was awarded the IPL TV rights for ten years for $1 billion (₹4500 crore), starting 2008. The BCCI cancelled the deal after the completion of IPL-1 in 2008 and asked for fresh bids for nine years from 2009. Sony went to court but was unsuccessful. Modi was able to show violations – for instance, deliveries being 'missed' in the live telecast. As a result, Sony was forced to bid again. It won, but at a cost of $1.8 billion (₹8100 crore) for nine years. I have rarely seen any 'missing' ball in the IPL telecast after that. But, of course, there were other 'innovations' – like ads on the sightscreen.

Ticket Fiasco

My fourth complaint is about the difficulty of buying match tickets – the problem became worse during World Cup 2011, for which Kyazoonga.com had been appointed as the official

[2] http://www.espncricinfo.com/south-africa-v-india-2010/content/story/498445.html

online ticketing agent. The first phase of ticket sales was launched on 1 June 2010 and on 3 June, I bought tickets for a few matches up to the quarter finals. The tickets for the semi-final and the final were supposed to go on sale later. Kyazoonga had been updating on their website that the tickets would be couriered by early February; eventually I got them on 9 March, just three days before the crucial India–South Africa match.

I also signed up for an 'alert' with Kyazoonga regarding tickets for the semi-final and the final. There was no news for months. Finally, a couple of days after the start of the WC on 19 February, I got an email about the online option. Within five minutes of the start of the sales online, the Kyazoonga website crashed as they vastly underestimated the potential demand for the tickets. After this fiasco, they (with agreement from BCCI and ICC) decided to go for a 'lucky draw' ballot – of a mere 1000 tickets available for the final. The fundamental issue is that most of the tickets – 20,000 – had been reserved for MCA (Mumbai Cricket Association) and for the ICC commercial partners (7900 tickets), leaving only 4000 tickets for the fans (including the thousand made available online).

Fortunately, I learnt in December 2010 that the ICC and the BCCI had decided that fans could buy match tickets for the semi-final in Mohali and final in Mumbai only with a 'package' – with odds and ends like high tea and memorabilia, and that only a small number of tickets would be available online. Though I didn't want any of these other things, I had no choice but to buy 'packages' for the semi-final and final; I bought such packages from Tui, an official ICC agent. When I got the semi-final ticket in Mohali on 30 March I realized that the ticket price itself was only ₹1000 but that I had paid ₹16,000 for the package. An official ICC T-Shirt with Tui's logo, tea and biscuits, and the option to use the bus to the stadium and back (which I didn't use) was worth ₹15,000! Similarly, on 2 April, I realized that the ticket price for the final was ₹15,000 but that I had paid ₹38,000 for the package. Was this sheer robbery or was this an example of 'breakthrough marketing innovation'?

But there was worse in store. In Bangalore, there was 'lathicharge' on fans who were disappointed that they couldn't get tickets despite having stood in the queue since the previous night. I guess I should consider myself lucky – being forced to buy a package is nothing in comparison to being beaten by the police![3]

The matters of delayed distribution of the tickets, the fiasco of the online site crash and overall disastrous management of the ticketing process made the ICC send an angry letter to Sharad Pawar as the chairman of the World Cup Central Organizing Committee (despite the fact that he was the ICC chairman).[4]

My fifth grouse is that the BCCI could not ensure the completion of the renovation of the Eden Gardens stadium in time for the 2011 World Cup, and that the ICC was forced to move the India–England match to another venue. The decision was warranted; clearly, we have not learnt from the CWG 'last-minute' syndrome and its ills. The responsibility of the stadium is that of the Cricket Association of Bengal (CAB), not that of the BCCI directly, but as an Indian cricket fan, the failure shames me.

As we have articulated through the book, consumer marketing is focused on the consumer and sports marketing,

[3] http://www.espncricinfo.com/icc_cricket_worldcup2011/content/current/story/502723.html

[4] http://sports.ndtv.com/world-cup-2011/news/item/169512-sharad-pawar-gets-angry-letter-from-icc-over-world-cup-tickets

on the fan. Great consumer marketing companies treat the consumer as the 'boss' in their thinking and action. But does the BCCI care about the Indian cricket fan? Does it have a vision for cricket in India?

Conclusions

Lessons for Sports Marketers

We conclude with ten suggestions for sports marketers – sponsors, media houses and especially cricket administrators – on how they can connect better with fans and grow their business.

Indian cricket administrators are in a triumphalist mode. Having seen off the challenge of domestic sports like football and hockey, they are now alone at the top of the pyramid. But being at the summit for too long brings altitude sickness. Although Indian cricket has done a fantastic commercial job, any sport that does not see fans as their reason for existence will not stay on top for long. There are warning signs that excessive focus on commercial output is compromising the fan experience. Our suggestions are to be seen in that regard – enhance the fan experience and prosper.

Focus on Fans, Reduce Reliance on TV

Franchises cost a lot of money and the way they expect to get their returns is through a share of the media and central sponsorships and additional local sponsorships they are able to rustle up. Since the media deals and central sponsorships are fixed by the BCCI and since ticketing revenues are still small, the opportunity for a local franchisee to make money lies in more merchandise, more local sponsorships and more local fan events. All these call for an active creation of a strong local fan base as opposed to the more passive media-focused strategy where central media and sponsorships target mainstream consumers – even those who are interested in IPL not for its cricket but entertainment value. Let the IPL target all consumers vaguely interested in cricket, but the franchisees should target fans.

An analysis of IPL club economics in the *Economic Times* on 29 April 2010 showed that 52 per cent of the revenues of a club come from TV rights and advertisements between overs at the stadium. For broadcasters to recover their money quickly, the easiest way is more advertisements. However, this is not a sustainable solution to their search for profitability, as fans get turned off by an overdose of advertising. The strategic approach would be for the BCCI and the broadcaster to increase the number of fans watching the game, both in India and abroad which will lead to the same advertisements commanding higher valuations.

Readers might recall the PwC report we talked about in the Prologue. The report analyses sources of revenue from sports marketing by source (gate – 38 per cent, media rights – 20 per cent, sponsorships – 26 per cent and merchandising – 16 percent), by regions (North America – 48 per cent, Europe, Middle East and Africa – 35 per cent, Asia Pacific – 15 per cent and Latin America – 2 per cent). The point is that worldwide, media rights provide only 20 per cent of revenues, whereas fan-focused revenue streams add up to 54 per cent (gate plus merchandise) making the franchise less vulnerable to the whims of the faddist consumer and the tactical media buyer.

The Deloitte 2008 Annual Review of Football Finance reported the revenue break-up for leading football club Manchester United as:

Tickets	39 per cent
Television	36 per cent
Merchandise/ sponsorships	25 per cent

In comparison to this, the assessment in the *Economic Times* (referred to above) for an IPL Club (season 3) would be:

TV – 45 per cent. Plus advertisements between overs on the ground (which find their way to our sets): another 7 per cent. Total 52 per cent

Internet rights – 5 per cent

Sponsorships (central) – 20 per cent

Ground sponsorships, blimp and hoardings – 7 per cent

Remainder – tickets, content deals, prize money, parties etc.

As the comparison shows, in India the problem for franchises is the overwhelming dependence on television for revenues. We do not watch sports to see the advertisements. Granted that some advertisements are necessary to keep the game going, but what is happening currently is a travesty of the game.

Build Loyalty by Improving Fan Experience

The New Meadowlands stadium, home of the New York Giants and New York Jets, is a spectacular sporting venue with plush interiors and restaurants, giant replay screens, and a mix of private boxes and general seats so that the in-stadium needs of regular fans as well as corporates are met. However, the stadium does not meet one of the core needs of fans – to get in and out of the stadium quickly. Thus there are traffic jams outside the stadium. Less focus on the optics and more on the simple needs of fans would have helped.

The Lord's stadium in London focuses on fans quite well with a museum, a book shop and a rest and recreation area; and similarly, the Melbourne Cricket Ground does a good job with a guided tour, and on match days, it provides extra tram services.

Watching cricket in India is, however, far from a pleasant experience. The weather, the crowds, the unhygienic conditions, the difficulty of entering and exiting the stadium, all tend to put off families. At some point the administrators will need to consider increasing the size of stadiums and converting large parts of the stadiums into air-conditioned boxes for family or business use, and charge accordingly. Some of the main stadia were constructed in the 1970s – for example, the M. Chinnaswamy Stadium in 1970–71 and the Wankhede Stadium in 1973 – with the assumption that 40,000 seats would be sufficient. However, the fan base and purchasing power has grown considerably since then. As Anil Kumble stated in February 2011 after the Bangalore World Cup ticketing fiasco: 'It's a matter of supply and demand.' The demand from fans for marquee events is well in excess of the stadium capacity.

Create International Demand

A report in *The Independent* on 2 April 2010 said that the IPL had made headway in the UK with IPL-3 getting approximately 0.5 million viewers for its Sunday games (even overtaking the England–Bangladesh Test viewership on the same day by 0.35 million). However, these numbers are still small compared to the 7.4 million viewers that the Ashes final got in 2005. Or the 143 million that IPL-3 got in India.

The NRI audience has increased dramatically over time and should not be ignored. Indian diaspora in the US, UK,

Southeast Asia are all prime targets for the IPL. Arranging club exhibition matches in places like Singapore or Kuala Lumpur will increase the fan base.

Bring Sporting Insights

It is increasingly obvious that brands are merging into each other in the clutter that accompanies an ODI or a Twenty20 telecast. How can companies make their brands distinctive in this clutter?

There are some Indian companies that have demonstrated great sports insights.

NIIT's sponsorship of Vishwanathan Anand sets them apart from other IT educators as they have an ambassador who embodies intelligence and application. The sporting insight is that chess helps develop concentration and can strengthen the mind.

NIIT's 'Mindchampions' initiative 2002–10 with Anand has reached 850,000 young chess players through grassroots tournaments.

Dara Singh, the famous Indian wrestler who also had a successful career in film and television, was synonymous with strength. VIP apparels '*mazboot itni*, *Dara Singh jitni*' was a smart way of communicating the product's benefit of strength and durability by using the wrestler as a benchmark.

Narain Karthikeyan's association with JK Tyres also makes perfect sense as one of the first things one associates with F1 is the screech of the tyres being put to test at high speeds. We have seen Formula 1 events in a number of countries and can attest to the fact that you can hear a Formula 1 event long before you reach the venue because of the distinctive sound of the tyres.

Let's look at some examples from Euro 2008.

Some of the major sponsors of Euro 2008 were Adidas, Carlsberg, Coca Cola, Hyundai, Austrian Post, Hublot (watches), Unicredit and Ferrero (the confectionary company).

They executed their marketing campaigns very differently based on consumer or sporting insights. Some of these were:

Adidas' attention to detail in designing the tournament ball, which would need a chapter in itself – suffice to say it was a masterpiece in design.

Carlsberg offered fans the opportunity to give away the man of the match award rather than have some company official hog the camera; in addition, their advertising campaign leveraged an insight that beer and football went together.

Coca Cola's innovation was in bringing fans to the team warm-ups.

Hyundai used the opportunity to create awareness and trial behind one of its offers – the Kia car.

McDonalds connected with kids by getting them to lead players onto the pitch.

Austrian Post set up special post offices for the event and advertised their association with it on their entire fleet of over 20,000 vehicles. Austrian Post also released a number of stamps (about forty) for the event.

Hublot launched a special 45-minute watch for referees and in a classy gesture, donated their hoardings for the 'United against Racism' campaign. Their sponsor hoardings on the side of the ground (perimeter boards) were used to create awareness about the campaign instead of displaying Hublot watches or their logo.

Persist with Brand Ambassadors

Brands tend to change sports properties they are associated with, and they do so too quickly. It is more important, in our opinion, for a brand to have someone who stands for a quality attribute like performance. A brand should neither panic when the brand ambassador loses on the field, nor celebrate excessively when he or she wins.

In India, Boost (the health milk drink) from Glaxo Smith Kline is one brand which has combined both continuity and change behind the single-minded proposition that '*Boost gives you more energy*.' In 1986, when Kapil was at his energetic best, Boost was the secret of his energy. When Sachin Tendulkar burst on to international cricket in 1991, the Boost ad featured both Kapil and Sachin proclaiming that Boost was the secret of their energy. Later, Sachin became the brand's lead ambassador. And in 2001, Sehwag was roped in with Sachin to proclaim the same message. It is a very impressive accomplishment for a brand to maintain one message and one campaign for over two decades. One interesting aside: one of the Kapil Dev advertisements featured a young boy. That boy was Nikhil Chopra, and he would go on to represent India in cricket. If Boost made one mistake, it was dropping Kapil a bit too early. They looked at age demographically, not psychographically. In the early 1990s, Kapil was still in his early thirties. Companies and marketers get bored of their brand ambassadors long before the fans (consumers) do.

It's Not Just about Cricket

As the Indian market grows there will be aggressive attempts by sports such as football, basketball and motorsport to penetrate the market. A clear option to cricket will be football, which till now has been event focused (World Cup) and geographically focused (East Zone, Goa and Kerala). More and more companies and sponsors will invest in football as the price tag on cricket rises. The 2010 FIFA World Cup generated an estimated ₹150 crore in advertising revenue in India – almost three times that of the 2006 World Cup. According to TAM India, the English Premiership had 28 million viewers in 2007, and 33 million viewers in 2008. Independent ESPN sources estimate EPL viewership at 39 million in 2010. Its success in other Asian markets would indicate that it has the potential to succeed in India. On the other hand we are less optimistic about local football like the Santosh Trophy and Federation Cup as viewers are more likely to watch international football because of the high standards of the game and the celebrity footballers.

Business-to-Business Opportunity

The Barclays English Premiership example covers both business-to-consumer (fans) and business-to-business areas (corporate hospitality). In India, as stadium facilities improve, the B2B opportunity will grow proportionately. The current stadia are small and too many sponsor boxes will create a backlash because fans will feel they are being cut out from the action. Larger stadia which can cater to fan demand and corporates are needed. Sponsor boxes are sometimes criticized by commentators, who tend to look at 'regular' fans more positively (some form of reverse snobbery), but franchises, brands and stadia all need the B2B component. The B2B opportunity covers trade, distributors and associations who influence or control the purchase decision.

Sports marketing in India is having to make choices between space for corporates and space for fans, which should not be the case.

Link Sponsorship to Brand Proposition

Rolex, the makers of possibly the world's best-known watch brand, have used sports achievements and contexts to highlight precision, reliability and luxury. What gives the brand some of its mystique is its presence at some of the great human achievements (it was on the wrist of Tenzing Norgay, the first man to climb Mt Everest in 1953), and exploration of the deepest oceans (the Mariana Trench on the wrist of Jacques Piccard in 1960).

What we find instructive is the consistent relationship that Rolex has established between precision and sport in a luxury brand context. Beyond breaking records (rather, recording firsts!), Rolex has later used sports endorsements through events (Tennis – Wimbledon, Australian Open; Golf – Ladies Professional Golf Association; Motor sports – Rolex Sports Car Series; Yachting – Rolex Cup etc.), sportsmen (Roger Federer, Lance Armstrong, to name just two).

One company which has linked their sponsorship to their brand and indeed the company's proposition is the IT company Mahindra Satyam. They are interested in gaining share in the logistics side of sport. Their 2010 FIFA World Cup sponsorship created awareness for their brand globally and provided proof that their technology works at a massive event.

Sports marketing has sufficient flexibility to cover mass and premium products, performance and precision, and B2C and B2B. But it needs to be relevant.

Brand Ambassadors Carry Risks

This is going against conventional wisdom, which is that your brand ambassador must embody the values of the brand. Brand ambassadors are human. For the most part they are successful, subjected to temptations you will never be subject to. The more brand ambassadors you have the greater the risk you incur. Sporting events too can be beset by scandals like match-fixing, drug abuse and other forms of cheating. That's why it's best to keep the connection more rational than stray into the area of an ambassador espousing the company's values. The moment you say a brand ambassador embodies your brand's values off the field it is like tempting fate.

Having a Bold Leader Helps

In our study on sports marketing, we frequently encounter this phenomenon. A visionary founder (such as Phil Knight of Nike), an entrepreneurial organization, the evolution of a new consumer need and a team that can connect it all and execute on the ground – this combination succeeds wildly.

It is well documented how Nike transformed the humble sneaker into something that provided 'authentic athletic performance' and then relentlessly got top athletes to use and recommend its products.

The spirit of adventure is common to business and sport. Companies that use a lot of data in decision-making to avoid any marketing risk sometimes go very wrong in sports marketing, which requires an intuitive understanding of fans and sport.

Sports marketing, like sports, has adventure, fun, unpredictability and risk built into it.

More than anything else, Indian cricket needs to realize that as the source of more than 70 per cent of world's cricket revenues, it needs to behave like a leader. For several years Indian cricket administrators and players were at the receiving end. Cricket fans in the 1980s may remember a disgraceful banner at the India–Pakistan finals of the 1985 Benson &

Hedges One-day tournament in Melbourne: 'Bus conductors vs. Tram Drivers'. Well, today, Indian cricket owns the bus, the tram, the stadium and is auctioning players, but it should use the power to create a vibrant, well-governed sports market. Leadership is about looking forward, not being vengeful about the past.

Indian cricket needs to recognize that with leadership come responsibilities – for example, helping teams like the West Indies recover from their general slump – with financial aid, if necessary. When England was at the centre of the cricket world upto the mid-1970s, it spread the game through much of the Commonwealth. Australia was the leader of cricket from the mid-1970s to 1990 and in this phase it took the sport forward through commercializing and marketing cricket, especially the One-day variety, through Kerry Packer and Channel Nine, and retaining the fans' loyalties for Test matches with the Ashes and the Border-Gavaskar Trophy. Leadership has now unquestionably passed to India as the epicentre of world cricket.

What will our legacy be?

Acknowledgements

Our sincere thanks to:

Sam Balsara, Harsha Bhogle, Anuja Chauhan, Sandeep Goyal, Brett Lee, Siddharta Mukherjee and S. Venkatraghavan, for sharing their insightful views and thoughts.

Melroy and Yasmin for helping with the interviews.

Amit Agarwal and Natasha Puri for the meticulous editing and Shuka Jain for the design aspects of the book.

Our respective families and friends who have been incredibly supportive.

Index